Created
to
Praise

Created
to
Praise

Derek Prime

CHRISTIAN
FOCUS

Scripture quotations taken from *the Holy Bible, New International Version*. Copyright © 1973, 1978, 1984 by International Bible Society.Used by permission of Hodder & Stoughton Publishers, A member of the Hodder Headline Group. All rights reserved. 'NIV' is a registered trademark of International Bible Society. UK trademark number 1448790.

After serving churches in the UK as a pastor for thirty years – first at Lansdowne Evangelical Free Church, West Norwood, in London and then at Charlotte Chapel in Edinburgh – Derek Prime has devoted himself since 1987 to an itinerant ministry and to writing.

Copyright © Derek Prime 2013

paperback ISBN 978-1-78191-236-2
epub ISBN 978-1-78191-239-3
Mobi ISBN 978-1-78191-240-9

10 9 8 7 6 5 4 3 2 1

First published in 1981

Reprinted in 1991 and 2013
by
Christian Focus Publications Ltd,
Geanies House, Fearn,
Ross-shire, IV20 1TW, Scotland.
www.christianfocus.com

Cover design
by
Daniel van Straaten

Printed by
Bell and Bain, Glasgow

MIX
Paper from
responsible sources
FSC
www.fsc.org
FSC® C007785

CONTENTS

Acknowledgements

The author wishes to thank Michael Baughen, Gustav Bosse Verlag and Sheldon Vanauken for permission to quote from their works.

INTRODUCTION

Two strangers once found themselves on the same ship. They began to watch one another closely, both conscious of an instinctive bond. But they came from different lands, and neither understood a word of the other's language.

On the Sunday they attended a church service in the ship's saloon. Each knew that the other could not follow the prayers, and each recognised the mutual desire to worship that had drawn them there.

That afternoon they sat, not far from one another, under the awning of the promenade deck. One of them noticed that the other had a Bible in his hand. He could remain silent no longer.

'Hallelujah!' he said, approaching his fellow traveller and pointing to the Bible.

'Amen,' the other smiled. They shook hands.

That little story is told by F.W. Boreham in *A Reel of Rainbow*. He notes that the men 'had found a meeting-place and a greeting-place among the monumental untranslatables.'

'Hallelujah' is that kind of untranslatable word – a word which occupies a unique place in international Christian vocabulary, a word by which Christians all over the world can communicate.

'Hallelujah' or 'Praise the Lord!' sums up my life's proper goal: the bringing of praise to the God who has made me, and also redeemed me by His Son Jesus Christ.

Provocative words started me off on this theme – the words, in fact, of Psalm 102:18: 'Let this be written for a future generation, that *a people not yet created may praise the LORD.*' The writer of the psalm looked forward to the time when Israel would be gathered out of the lands of her exile and be made once more into a people of the Lord. God Himself speaks of His people in this way, through the prophet Isaiah, when He declares, 'The people I formed for myself that they may proclaim my praise' (Isa. 43:21). Sadly, Israel lost sight at times of her destiny as an instrument for God's praise. As a Christian I may, unfortunately, do the same.

I want to try to establish the right position of praise in the Christian's life, because praise occupies a unique place in God's purposes. When God first formed man, man was created to praise God; when we are born again, through faith in our Lord Jesus Christ, we are *recreated* in order that we may praise God.

And yet – if we are frank – we do not always find it easy to praise God, much as we may want to do so. We must not pretend that such difficulties do not exist. They are certainly not unique, and they are probably much more common than we think. We need to face up to problems so that we genuinely seek after answers God may graciously choose to provide.

So what exactly did the Old Testament writers mean by 'praise'? Top of the list comes *Hillel,* meaning *cry aloud* or *break out into a cry and especially a cry of joy.* It conveys the thought of making a noise! So great is the Lord that His people must draw attention to His glory. He is 'worthy of praise' (2 Sam. 22:4).

'Shout for joy to the LORD, all the earth,' Psalm 100 begins, and that exhortation does not stand on its own (e.g. Ps. 98:4, 6; Zeph. 3:14; Zech. 9:9 etc). And yet some people may feel that there is something almost undignified and out of place about loud and demonstrative praise, or that warm demonstrations of our feelings are contrary to our culture or temperament. We may even try to 'shout for joy' in a muffled and polite mumble!

But we should be prepared to challenge our caution and reserve with the Bible's plain exhortations. Loud praise is consistently associated with joy in God. When we are excited about ordinary things we tend to raise our voices. When something wonderful happens, we often talk about it loudly. As God graciously reveals glimpses of His glory, or renews our experience of His deliverance, it is natural for us to express our praise with intensity and volume.

Of course, there is no virtue whatsoever in loud praise just for the sake of noise and its loudness is no guarantee of its reality. But we must not be afraid to express the depths of our feelings as we worship God. If we raise our voices in praise and welcome of some important state dignitary, should we not raise our voices at the presence of the King of kings and Lord of lords? Even as there is variation in tempo and volume in a beautiful piece of music, so there will be variation in the expression of our praise to God. What is important is that we should not be inhibited in expressing sincere praise. Loud praise should never be 'put on'; it must always be an unaffected burst of delight in God Himself, too great to be constrained.

John Wesley, the founder of Methodism, was concerned that people's praise should be enthusiastic:

> Sing lustily, and with a good courage ... Beware of singing as if you were half dead or half asleep; but lift up your voice with strength. Be no more afraid of your voice now, nor more ashamed of its being heard, than when you sang the songs of Satan.

There is no danger of our being over-enthusiastic in our praise of God if it is from our heart. The soul that is in love with Jesus Christ must sing! 'What are our lame praises in comparison of His love?' asked Archbishop Leighton. And his answer was: 'Nothing, and less than nothing; but love will stammer rather than be dumb.'

A PRAYER

Lord, too often I've failed to praise You. Sometimes I haven't wanted to praise You for reasons I've been unwilling to admit to myself. On other occasions I've not praised You properly, and yet I've wanted to do so.

I quietly remember before You now that you have created me, and You have redeemed me through the Lord Jesus Christ, that I might proclaim Your praise.

Teach me how to praise You as I ought. Deliver me from any unhelpful inhibitions arising from either my natural temperament or the culture or traditions which have moulded my life. Help me to stammer rather than be dumb. Make the praise of my lips to be more than matched by my praise of You in the life I live.

I ask these things for the glory of Your name.

Amen.

1

Man's Chief End

'Why am I here?' We all must have asked that question at times – and if not in those words, in others very similar. To understand man's chief end – the purpose of God's creation of man – we must appreciate God's design for the whole of creation, for man represents a significant part of that creation.

THE REVELATION OF GOD'S GLORY

'In the beginning God created the heavens and the earth' – that's how the Bible dramatically begins, and it must be our starting point. Every created thing traces its origin to God's will by which it was created (Rev. 4:11). The life we enjoy comes from Him, 'the fountain of life' (Ps. 36:9). He it was who created our inmost being and knit us together in our mother's womb (Ps. 139:13). If we ask, 'Why did God make us?' the Bible's answer finds its best summary in the Shorter Catechism: 'Man's chief end is to glorify God, and to enjoy Him for ever.' 'For from him and through him and to him are all things,' declares the Bible (Rom. 11:36).

Let's ponder those words: 'From him ... through him ... and to him are all things.' The importance of this statement cannot be exaggerated. It is not a fact we could have discovered for ourselves, but a truth which God carefully makes known to us as we honestly seek to understand both ourselves and the world around us. Greater even than God's revelation of Himself in nature or through the prophets is God's unique and final revelation of Himself in our Lord Jesus Christ (Heb. 1:1, 2), who is described as 'the image of the invisible God, the firstborn over all creation' (Col. 1:15).

God lets us into a great secret: not only did He create all things by His Son but also for Him (Col. 1:16). Creation, therefore, finds its reason for existence in God alone; and man discovers his own reason for existence only as he learns to praise his Creator, and particularly as he learns to praise his Creator through Jesus Christ (Heb. 13:15).

No higher end

Some argue against God's glory being man's chief end because they feel it contains some unworthy suggestion of selfishness on God's part. But this argument arises from a misunderstanding. Whenever we, as sinful men and women, try to make or achieve anything, our human selfishness inevitably creeps into it. Others may rival us or we may simply want to make a name for ourselves. But it is the height of human presumption to judge God by our human standards, although our finiteness and perversity easily lead us into that trap.

One truth we must firmly grasp – God is perfect. And from His perfection there follows the profound truth that God can have no higher end than Himself. We as creatures are limited. All that we accomplish, no matter how admired by our fellow creatures, bears the stamp of our finiteness. Our Creator, however, stands apart, entirely different, and He alone is worthy of the worship of His whole creation.

As Martin Luther expressed it, when commenting on Psalm 84:4-6:

> Since we receive everything from God, there is nothing that we can render Him but praise, and praise to Him alone. For a person cannot praise God only, unless he understands that there is nothing in himself worthy of praise, but that all that is worthy of praise is of God and from God. But since God is eternally praiseworthy, because He is the infinite Good and can never be exhausted, therefore they will praise Him for ever and ever.

In heaven, where God's redeemed creatures grasp the whole truth, they proclaim to the Lord: 'You are worthy, our Lord and God, to receive glory and honour and power, for you created all things, and by your will they were created and have their being' (Rev. 4:11).

The first chapter of Genesis, in fact, constitutes a call to praise God, although the word 'praise' is not mentioned once. Every time the narrative declares God seeing 'that it was good', we should be declaring 'Hallelujah!'

When studying the theme of praise in the Bible it is important not to limit ourselves to the occasions when the word itself is used. Let me illustrate what I mean. When my children were younger and did their homework well, I could have said, 'I praise you!' However, put that way the use of the word 'praise' sounds rather stilted. On the other hand, I could look at their work and say, 'That's very good!' and such would have been equally praise. Every time the Bible points out God's excellences to us, we are called to praise Him.

While on the one hand our praise must never lack reverence, it must not, on the other hand, become stilted and be marked by archaic formality. Reality is a principal factor. One Sunday I was about to drive home after church and a young man called Tony, who was a new Christian, came racing up to me on his bicycle. I thought he had perhaps left something behind after the morning service, and wanted me to open the church for him to get it. 'What is it, Tony?' I asked. 'Isn't the Lord wonderful!' was his reply. God's Word had so come home to his mind and heart that morning that he wanted to share it with me. Was that not true praise of the Lord? I've come to appreciate that my spiritual life is at a low ebb if there are no times when I say to the Lord, 'You are wonderful!' and when I want to say to other Christians, 'Isn't the Lord great?'

MAN'S UNIQUENESS

Man was created last by God as the terminus and summit of the creatures brought into being to inhabit the world (Gen. 1:26, 27). He alone was made in the image of God – a personal, moral, free and rational spirit. From the beginning man was able to appreciate the wonders of God's creation and was called upon to undertake one of the earliest scientific tasks in the world – the naming of every creature. 'Whatever the man called each living creature, that was its name' (Gen. 2:19b). Adam possessed all the knowledge that we, thousands of years later, have to strive after with difficulty. Adam was able to give suitable names to all of God's creatures according to their respective natures. Plato once remarked that the wisest man was the man who first gave appropriate names to things. If, for example, we got together the wisest men and the most erudite scientists, and gave them the task of giving accurate, descriptive names to all of God's creatures, we would gain some idea of the vast wisdom with which Adam was endowed by God.

With his judgement as yet unmarred by sin, man stood in a unique position to appreciate God's purpose in each creature's creation and to perceive God's perfections in His creative work. 'For since the creation of the world God's invisible qualities – his eternal power and divine nature – have been clearly seen, being understood from what has been made' (Rom. 1:20) – and Adam was able to respond to God in praise and fellowship as he appreciated the wonders of God's creation and all it reveals of God's character. The Greek word for man is *anthropos*. It is interesting to note that popular Greek etymology declared that anthropos meant the 'upward looker'.

An intelligent being, unspoiled by transgression, Adam was able to boast in God. He was wise enough to look away from himself to God as the source of all good. His joy hinged not upon himself but upon all God was to him. His true praise of God exercised itself as he lived a life of fellowship with God – God walked in the garden in the cool of the day (Gen. 3:8) – and Adam responded to his Creator first in admiration and worship, and then in loving care of the work of God's hands. As Adam ruled over God's creation, reflecting God's perfect care and concern for it, he brought glory to God as a diligent son does to a worthy father.

THE TRAGEDY OF THE FALL

We begin to see how great, therefore, was the tragedy of man's fall. Man, in effect, cast doubt upon the perfection of his own creation – he wanted to be different from what he was. 'You will be like God' was the serpent's tempting promise (Gen. 3:5). Man cast doubt upon the perfection of God's character as he accepted Satan's insinuations about God's motives in barring man from the tree of the knowledge of good and evil. '"You will not certainly die," the serpent said to the woman. "For God knows that when you eat from it your eyes will be opened, and you will be like God, knowing good and evil"' (Gen. 3:4, 5).

Praise of God and genuine trust in Him go hand in hand. When we praise God we acknowledge how good and faithful He is and much else besides, and that is why we can trust Him so completely. Furthermore, wholehearted trust in God must include trusting Him when He doesn't choose to reveal the reasons for His prohibitions or His manner of doing things. As man trusts God, without always understanding God's ways, his fellowship with God grows deeper – and through that deeper fellowship, greater understanding develops (cf. Ps. 73:16, 17). Often we trust in order to understand. But man in the beginning succumbed to the temptation to doubt God, and cast aside the fellowship for which he was made and in which lay his safety and his key to knowledge.

Adam found himself immediately on a slippery slope. Justly driven out of the Garden of Eden (Gen. 3:22-24) and no longer able to enjoy close fellowship with God, man further frustrated the object of his creation – he made himself the object of praise. Instead of wanting to make much of God, he began to make much of himself.

When men began to build the tower of Babel, they said, 'Come, let us build ourselves a city, with a tower that reaches to the heavens, so that we may make a name for ourselves ...' (Gen. 11:4). Their purpose was self-glorification. Man became a boaster (Ps. 52:1; 94:4), focused his attention on himself and no longer looked up to God; he trusted in himself instead of having confidence in God (Jer. 9:23, 24). We share in man's folly, and I think we would have understood it if God had simply chosen to 'write off' the whole of His creation. But He didn't.

THE AMAZING WISDOM OF GOD

We gain an insight here into the amazing wisdom of God in the plan of redemption. God conceived a plan by which man could be restored to God – including being restored to God's original purpose of being created for His praise – with even more cause to praise Him and to live for His praise than at the beginning.

But the timing of the revelation of this plan of redemption had to be absolutely right, and preparation was necessary if the world was to appreciate it when God made it known. God made a beginning with Abraham when He chose the Jewish people as those to whom He would reveal both Himself and also His plan. To this people it was said, 'He is your praise' (Deut. 10:21). They were to praise Him, initially, as no other nation because of their unique enjoyment of God's self-revelation. '"For as a belt is bound around a man's waist, so I bound the whole house of Israel and the whole house of Judah to me," declares the LORD, "to be my people for my renown and praise and honour" ' (Jer. 13:11). The Jewish people fell short of God's purposes all too often, but they knew that God's pre-eminent purpose in their creation as a people was for His praise.

As a race the Jews were the means God used for achieving His redemptive purpose. By signs and symbols He prepared the way for the coming of the Saviour. The Old Testament Scriptures, which God entrusted to the Jews, proclaimed the Person and work of the promised Messiah (1 Pet. 1:10-12). And when the right time came, and the Messiah was born, He was born into a Jewish home.

But God's purpose always extended beyond the Jewish people, slow as the majority of Jews were to appreciate it. The initial promise Abram received contained within it the great and ultimate design of God – 'all peoples on earth will be blessed through you' (Gen. 12:3).

THE PRAISE THE GOSPEL GENERATES

Today, as in the centuries before us, men and women of all races learn to praise God on account of the gospel of our Lord Jesus Christ. They become God's new Israel – and, as such, they are *created for praise*. Our Lord's birth itself illustrated the praise that was to come. Mary's song began with the words, 'My soul glorifies the Lord ...' (Luke 1:46), and Zechariah, able to speak again after John's birth, spoke again with the words, '*Praise be to the Lord*, the God of Israel, because he has come to his people and has redeemed them' (Luke 1:68). Having witnessed the coming into the world of the Messiah as a baby, 'the shepherds returned *glorifying and praising God* for all the things they had heard and seen, which were just as they had been told' (Luke 2:20).

As the preface to an 1818 hymnbook declares,

The dispensation under which we live, was introduced to the notice of mankind by praise – and by praise from those who could not be supposed to taste, as we may, 'redeeming grace and dying love'. No sooner had the angel announced 'the good tidings of great joy', than a multitude of the heavenly host took up the theme, and, by turning it into a song, discovered how much they felt interested in the subject. Instantaneously they united, and sang in company, not singly; and magnified Jehovah, not merely with a simple elevation of their spiritual nature, but audibly, by voice, in the air.

As Simeon later took up the child in his arms, he too 'praised God' (Luke 2:28) and Anna, likewise, 'gave thanks to God' (Luke 2:38).

The spontaneity of their worship is something to covet and emulate. Of course, the circumstances of God's revelation to them were unique. But when the awareness of these same glorious events – and many others besides – come home to us, we should not be slow in expressing our worship and praise. Spontaneity is much more easily expressed, of course, in private or in small groups. But those who lead the corporate praise of God's people perhaps need to recognise that it is good to depart sometimes from what we have prayerfully planned, if the teaching and preaching of God's Word brings home some aspect of God's character and dealings with His people which calls for specific and immediate praise. If those who lead corporate praise are filled with the Spirit, they will be sensitive to the desire for corporate praise on the part of their fellow-members of the body of Christ.

Jews and Gentiles, redeemed alike by the blood of Christ, know themselves to be a 'chosen people, a royal priesthood, a holy nation, a people belonging to God, that [they] may declare the praises of him who called [them] out of darkness into his wonderful light' (1 Pet. 2:9).

Reconciled to God through Jesus Christ, we praise Him with a new understanding for His creation – with perhaps something akin to the understanding man had in the beginning. 'The heavens declare the glory of God' we affirm, and 'the skies proclaim the work of his hands' (Ps. 19:1).

Jonathan Edwards, the seventeenth-century pastor and theologian, relates his own experience:

> The appearance of everything was altered; there seemed to be, as it were, a calm, sweet cast, or appearance of divine glory, in almost everything. God's excellency, His wisdom, His purity and love, seemed to appear in everything, in the sun, moon and stars; in the clouds, and blue sky; in the grass, flowers, trees, in the water and all nature.

The day after his conversion D.L. Moody remembered:

> I thought the old sun shone a good deal brighter than it ever had before – I thought it was just smiling upon me; and as I walked out upon Boston Common and heard the birds singing in the trees, I thought they were all singing a song to me. Do you know, I fell in love with the birds. I had never cared for them before. It seemed to me that I was in love with all creation. I had not a bitter feeling against any man, and I was ready to take all men to my heart.

On the rugged slopes of Norway in the early part of the twentieth century a young boy of eight sought God's salvation. His name was Abraham Vereide. Years later, he wrote

> As I prayed, I had a vivid consciousness of a Divine Presence and into my mind flashed a statement that I later discovered was from Isaiah 43:1: 'Fear not, for I have redeemed thee and called thee by name, thou art mine.' I accepted that, not knowing what it meant but that God had undertaken for me, and I yielded Him my all, so far as I knew. With it came a sense of release, of peace and joy. I rose to my feet, and as I looked around, everything seemed to be so beautiful, the moss, the grass, the trees, the leaves, the sky above me, everything had taken on a different hue ...'

A father spoke the other day of the conversion of his twelve-year old son. 'It was as if he had swallowed a book of systematic theology. As we drove in the car through the countryside, he remarked on the trees and other works of nature, "Look, Dad, see what God made!"'

> Heaven above is softer blue,
> Earth around is sweeter green;
> Something lives in every hue
> Christless eyes have never seen:
> Birds with gladder songs o'erflow,
> Flowers with deeper beauties shine,
> Since I know, as now I know,
> I am His and He is mine.
> (G.W. Robinson)

But we praise God above all for His new creation in Jesus Christ (2 Cor 5:17), of which we have become part through our new birth! We can never praise Him enough for His grace and loving kindness in giving His only begotten Son to be our Saviour. As the ever-growing wonders of our being 'in Christ' daily dawn upon us, so our praise of God increases. We praise Him for His grace in the provision of daily forgiveness, and we long to show forth His praise in grateful living. Fulfilling in some measure our present chief end, we anticipate with excitement the enjoyment of God for ever.

A PRAYER

Father, You are worthy to receive glory and honour and power for from You, through You and to You are all things.

Thank You for helping me to understand that I only discover my real reason for existence as I learn to praise You through Jesus Christ, Your Son and my Saviour. I bow in wonder before Your amazing wisdom revealed in the plan of salvation, and I thank You that Your salvation has become real in my life.

Please keep on enlightening the eyes of my heart so that knowing You better I may praise You better. Help me to enjoy praising You so much that I may honestly anticipate the joys of heaven. I ask this for the praise of Your Name and in the Name of the Lord Jesus Christ.

Amen.

2

Praise's Preoccupation

Praise is man's legitimate and proper preoccupation with God. The late Senator Robert Kennedy visited Brazil and in the course of his trip was taken into the interior of the country to see some of the tribal situations. He was introduced, by interpretation, to an Indian who had not long been converted. 'Ask him,' the senator said to his interpreter, 'what does he enjoy doing most?' The Indian's reply came as a surprise, 'Being occupied with God.' Convinced that the Indian had not understood his question, and that the answer should have been something like fishing or hunting, the senator insisted the question be repeated, but the answer came back again – 'Being occupied with God.' This seemingly insignificant Indian, now part of God's new creation, had discovered his chief end in life.

GOD'S SELF-REVELATION
If God chose to remain hidden from man, man would be helpless to know anything about Him. God is sovereign, and He alone can determine what His creatures shall be

permitted to know and understand about Him. But in His graciousness God has revealed Himself to mankind and the Bible records that revelation with care and in detail – a revelation which reaches its culmination in our Lord Jesus Christ, in whose face we are given 'the light of the knowledge of the glory of God' (2 Cor. 4:6).

God is spirit, and He has no body. The revelation He gives of Himself is of His Name, or His character. When the Lord appeared to Abram – and we are not told in what manner – He said, 'I am God *Almighty*' (Gen. 17:1) and later He revealed Himself to Moses as 'I AM' (Exod. 3:14). A high-point in Moses' experience of God and God's revelation to him was when 'the Lord came down in the cloud and stood there with him and proclaimed His name, the LORD. And He passed in front of Moses, proclaiming, "The LORD, the LORD, the compassionate and gracious God, slow to anger, abounding in love and faithfulness, maintaining love to thousands, and forgiving wickedness, rebellion and sin"' (Exod. 34:5-7).

Today, we tend to use names somewhat thoughtlessly, and the personal names we possess – except perhaps the nick-names – bear little relationship to our character. But the opposite was the case among the Jews. Think for a moment of someone you love very much – perhaps your closest relative or best friend. If I now ask you to describe him or her, and why he or she means so much to you, would you begin by telling me of his or her physical appearance or would you talk in terms of character? I guess that almost certainly you would be sharing details of character. Now in Bible language what you would be telling me would be that person's *name* – his or her character as you know it to be, for sure.

The Lord proclaimed to Moses *His Name* – He is the Lord, compassionate, gracious, slow to anger, abounding in love and faithfulness (Exod. 34:6, 7). Just as the beams of the sun shine forth its glory, so these adjectives, describing God's character, are the beams by which God's divine nature shines forth so that we can know what He is like, learn to know Him, and respond in intelligent praise.

PRAISE AND THANKSGIVING

Praise's preoccupation is with who God is, whereas thanksgiving's preoccupation is with what God has done. Praise looks more to God's Person than to His gifts. We praise God for who He *is*; we thank Him for what He has *done*. We must not draw too rigid a distinction between praise and thanksgiving, however, because one passes over into the other, at times almost imperceptibly. Glorifying God and giving thanks to Him are virtually the same thing (Rom. 1:21). Praise attempts a description of God but never achieves it. But still it persists with what it knows is an impossible task.

PREOCCUPATION WITH THE NAME

It is no exaggeration to say that Old Testament praise occupies itself with the Name of God. God's Name – the sum of His self-revelation – constitutes the believer's assurance of protection and help. 'The name of the LORD is a strong tower; the righteous run to it and are safe' (Prov. 18:10). Whereas worshippers of heathen gods run to vain temples or bow before powerless idols of their own creation, true believers trust in God's Name, a fact which underlines the spiritual nature of God. Psalm 54, verses 1 and 6, provides a typical example: 'Save me, O God, by your name; vindicate me by your might ... I will sacrifice a freewill offering to you; I will praise your name, O LORD, for it is good.' God's Name – His self-revelation – gave the psalmist the assurance that God would be his strength and deliverer in times of trouble and that the Lord is good, which is another way of saying that He is in every way all that God ought to be. Not surprisingly, therefore, the praise of God in the Old Testament centres upon God's self-revelation, upon His Name.

'Glorify the LORD with me; let us exalt his name together,' urges David (Ps. 34:3). We might paraphrase his words as follows: 'Let's praise God by talking together about all He has revealed Himself to be, and then telling Him how much we appreciate Him for Himself, and how we reverence and love Him.' Praise and thanksgiving are called forth by almost countless revelations of God's goodness, but probably five aspects come to the fore. First there is God's majesty and power (1 Chron. 29:11f); second, His mighty acts in the history of His people (Ps. 105:1-6); third, His enduring love (Ps. 118:1-4); fourth, His saving of men from distress (Ps. 107); and fifth, His deliverance of His people from their enemies (Ps. 9:1ff).

THE NAME OF JESUS

We find exactly the same emphasis in the New Testament upon the significance of the Name. The Old Testament manner of speaking of God's Name is transferred to the Lord Jesus and His Name. The great significance of His life and activity is expressed by His Name: 'You are to give him the name Jesus, because he will save his people from their sins' (Matt. 1:21). The actual name 'Jesus' can be replaced simply by 'the name': 'The apostles left the Sanhedrin, rejoicing because they had been counted worthy of suffering disgrace for the Name' (Acts 5:41; cf. 3 John 7). In fact, the whole content of the saving truth revealed in Jesus is comprised in His Name, so that Peter declared before the Sanhedrin, 'Salvation is found in no one else, for there is no other name under heaven given to mankind by which we must be saved' (Acts 4:12).

> There's no greater Name than Jesus
> Name of him who came to save us,
> In that saving Name of Jesus
> Every knee should bow.
> (M.A. Baughen)

A Christian's whole life is controlled by the superiority of the name Jesus: 'And whatever you do, whether in word or deed, do it all in the name of the Lord Jesus, giving thanks to God the Father through him' (Col. 3:17).

God the Father's delight is that all men and women should praise the name of His Son, and in so doing they glorify the Father because He sent the Son into the world, and the Son reveals the Father to us (John 3:16, 17:6; Phil. 2:11). As the chorus expresses it:

> His name is Wonderful, His name is Wonderful,
> His name is Wonderful, Jesus my Lord.
> He is the mighty King, Master of everything,
> His name is Wonderful, Jesus my Lord.
> He's the great Shepherd,
> The Rock of all ages, Almighty God is He.
> Bow down before Him, love and adore Him,
> His name is Wonderful, Jesus my Lord.

We rejoice in God through our Lord Jesus Christ (Rom. 5:11; Phil. 3:2) and boasting in His Cross (Gal. 6:14) all self-praise disappears.

THE WAY TO PRAISE

Praise's proper preoccupation with the Name of God and the Name of Jesus, the second Person of the Trinity, leads us to a fundamental conclusion about praise: we need to meditate upon the attributes of God – another way of expressing God's Name. Meditation for most of us presents difficulties. I, for one, always seem to be dashing about from place to place, appointment to appointment, and from one responsibility to another. And when I sit down, or kneel to pray, my mind so quickly wanders over all that has preoccupied it in the preceding few hours. But the pace of life – reflected in the state of mind I've described – underlines the even greater importance of meditation.

To meditate is to think quietly of the Name of God – of His self-revelation in creation, the Scriptures, and supremely in His Son our Lord Jesus Christ – until our minds and hearts are lifted above earthly preoccupations to be totally preoccupied for a while with God Himself, causing worship, both silent and spoken, to well up within our souls, so that we fulfil part of our chief end as we find ourselves praising God.

But how to go about meditation is the main problem. An obvious way is to allow ourselves to be guided by the Scriptures we read. I would wholeheartedly recommend establishing the habit of daily Bible reading. For most of us it is a battle to maintain this habit effectively so that we really benefit from it daily. But its maintenance is part of the spiritual battle that the Christian life involves for every believer (Eph. 6:10-18) and our spiritual enemy Satan has something to do with many of the hindrances we find in our way. But if we are realistic and honest about this battle, we see all the more reason to determine to try and win it with God's help.

So let's imagine, for example, you are reading in the Book of Proverbs, and in chapter 3, verses 19 and 20, you read, 'By wisdom the LORD laid the earth's foundations, by understanding he set the heavens in place; by his knowledge the watery depths were divided, and the clouds let drop the dew.' Begin by picking out the things said about God Himself – His wisdom, His understanding and His knowledge. Now pause to think about them, first in relation to his creation – for that is the writer of Proverbs' subject here – and then in relationship to yourself. Ponder God's wisdom in the plan He has for your own life, His understanding of your temperament and difficulties, His knowledge of you which extends to your motives and your heart. It will not be long before you are praising Him!

'One must meditate on the works of God and consider them well,' declared Luther. 'Then one will discover how wonderful and great they are, and then the heart will find in them nothing but admiration, pleasure and joy.'

Daily reading of the Scriptures may not always direct our thoughts, however, to God's Name, and this alternative may help, which I have found beneficial in the past and feel in need of practising again. Write out on each page of a loose-leaf notebook an attribute of God. Then as you daily read the Scriptures and discover some verse or statement about God's character, add it to your notebook under the appropriate heading, perhaps writing it out in full. Then begin your time of prayer each day by pondering for a few moments one of God's attributes. Besides adding freshness to your praise and prayer, it will serve to increase your understanding of God and make your reading of the Bible more careful and discerning. I find it helpful also to add phrases, sentences or verses from hymns which express God's attributes.

I believe it is probably important that our findings should be very personal to us. But let me share with you my initial list of God's attributes, limiting myself to just one Scripture reference for each, so as to help you to get started. I would emphasise the fact, however, that my list is merely a beginning. It goes like this: God's goodness (Ps. 118; 1), kindness or covenant faithfulness and love (Ps. 25:10), holiness (Isa. 6:3), power (Deut. 3:24), glory (Eph. 1:17), grace (Eph.1:6), mercy (Rom. 15:9), wisdom (Rom. 11:33), justice (Rom. 11:33) and uniqueness (Ps. 71:16).

To these attributes I would then add the attention the New Testament draws to aspects of the Name of our Lord Jesus Christ – that is to say, to His character and His Person: His grace (Acts 15:11), His love (Rom. 8:35), His power (1 Cor. 5:4), His glory (2 Thess. 2:14), His meekness and gentleness (2 Cor. 10:1), His Kingship (Eph. 5:5), His Headship (Eph. 5:23), His affection (Phil. 1:8), His humility (Phil. 2:5ff), His Saviourhood (Phil. 3:20), His high priestly office (Heb. 3:1), His unchangeableness (Heb. 13:8) and His mercy (Jude 21). Once again, these suggestions provide only a beginning, but often that is all we need to get started.

THE REASONABLENESS OF THIS APPROACH

If we really love someone we will often think about that person, and to do so increases our appreciation and love. Loving God, we think about Him, and the Holy Spirit brings a new dimension to our appreciation and love for God as we set our thoughts on God's attributes.

What is more, the constantly renewed realisation of all that God is to us in Jesus Christ and how He manifests Himself to us awakens joy in our souls and draws forth renewed confidence in God as we appreciate that we are the chosen objects of His care. Then we can think of nothing better than being *created to praise*!

A PRAYER

I thank You, Father, for Your Name, that You are the Lord, compassionate, gracious, slow to anger, and abounding in love and faithfulness.

While I want to be unceasing in my thanksgiving to You for all you have done for me, and all You continually give me, help me to look more to all that You are in Yourself than even to Your wonderful gifts.

Thank You for making real to me by Your Spirit the preciousness of the name of Jesus. How I praise You for Him! Please forgive me that so often I don't give myself a chance to be still so as to think about Your greatness. I want to be still now. Show me Your glory and receive my worship as I bring my silent adoration and audible expressions of praise. May I know what it is to rejoice in You, my Father, and in Your Son who is my Saviour by the power of Your Spirit. Amen.

3

Praise in Song

'It is good to praise the LORD and make music to your name, O Most High, to proclaim your love in the morning and your faithfulness at night, to the music of the ten-stringed lyre and the melody of the harp. For you make me glad by your deeds, O LORD; I sing for joy at the works of your hands' – so begins Psalm 92.

God's people have always been a singing people, and God's deliverance has prompted their praise above everything else. When their flight from Egypt was completed Moses and the Israelites broke out into a song of praise to the Lord, beginning with the words 'I will sing to the LORD for he is highly exalted ...' (Exod. 15:1ff). 'Then Miriam the prophetess, Aaron's sister, took a tambourine in her hand, and the women followed her, with tambourines and dancing. Miriam sang to them: "Sing to the LORD, for he is highly exalted. The horse and its rider he has hurled into the sea" ' (Exod. 15:20, 21). And God's people have continued to be a singing people throughout the ages. It has been one of their distinguishing marks.

An invitation to sing is frequently found at the beginning of an Old Testament expression of praise. So, for example, the psalmist exhorts us, 'Give thanks to the LORD, call on his name; make known among the nations what he has done.' But he does not stop there. He continues, 'Sing to him, sing praise to him; tell of all his wonderful acts' (Ps. 105:1, 2; cf. Isa. 42:10). The two exhortations – 'Sing to the LORD!' and 'Give praise to the LORD!' are almost the same thing (Jer. 20:13). Singing is one of the most natural ways of expressing praise, and it has the power to increase the feelings of admiration and gratitude we feel to God.

GOD'S SINGING HOUSE

Dayuma, the Ecuadorian Indian girl who, having once escaped from the Aucas, the world's most murderous tribe, returned to them when she became a Christian and described a church in her native Auca language as 'God's singing house', and, although a church is much more than that, she pinpointed one of the principal characteristics of God's people.

I gain the impression from the New Testament that if we could have visited the early Christians we would have been struck by their joyfulness in the Lord. They sang psalms, hymns and spiritual songs with gratitude in their hearts to the Lord (Col. 3:16). Some have tried to differentiate between the three terms – psalms, hymns and spiritual songs - but it is probably impossible to do so with accuracy, and most likely we are not intended to do so. Taken together, they describe the full range of singing that the Spirit prompts.

PSALMS

Psalms are literally 'songs of praise to God', and were invariably accompanied by music. As Luther expressed it, 'A psalm is a song of praise or a laudatory poem such as the poets composed, sung in times past to the accompaniment of string music.' Psalm 145, for example, has as its title 'A Song of Praise', in other words a 'Hallelujah'. If we interpret the 'psalm' in terms of the verb from which the noun comes, a psalm is a song sung to the accompaniment of a stringed instrument.

HYMNS

Hymns are also expressions of praise to God, and for the most part the verb from which we obtain the noun is translated 'to extol' and 'to praise'.

Psalm 136 is an example of an Old Testament hymn. It begins with a three-part call for praise to God: 'Give thanks to the LORD ...' (1-3). It then recounts God's acts in creation (4-9). He is next praised and extolled as God's people's Liberator from Egypt and as their Helper during the wilderness period and the conquest (10-22). He is further praised as the Deliverer (23, 24), and as the Giver of daily sustenance (25). The call to worship is then taken up once more (26). In fact, all the Old Testament's principal themes of praise are found here. The second half of each verse in the psalm further underlines the element of praise with its chorus *His love endures for ever.* This refrain was probably sung by a second choir, or as a response by part of the gathered congregation. It was hymns such as this that Paul and Silas sang at midnight in the inner cell of the prison at Philippi (Acts 16:25).

SONGS

Spiritual songs are the expression of the gratitude in our hearts to God for what He has done for us in our Lord Jesus Christ (Col. 3:16), and they revolve around the Person of our Lord Jesus, His saving work and His present activity on behalf of His people. They express our response to the salvation God has given us in His Son. Filled with the Spirit, such spiritual songs come readily to our lips (Eph. 5:18, 19), and spiritual singing, that is, singing with the help of the Holy Spirit, provides us with a means of ministering to one another (Col. 3:16).

A SPIRITUAL TONIC

The singing of God's praise seems to be closely linked with our encouraging and urging right action upon one another. Paul exhorts the Ephesians: 'Speak to one another with psalms, hymns and spiritual songs. Sing and make music from your heart to the Lord, always giving thanks to God the Father for everything, in the name of our Lord Jesus Christ' (Eph. 5:19, 20). Now he could be suggesting that by singing the actual words of Scripture and the sayings of the Lord Jesus Christian believers may exhort one another to right action. So, for example, if we sing the words of the Lord Jesus, 'Everyone will know that you are my disciples if you love one another' (John 13:35), we do, in fact, exhort one another to do this, and at the same time we write these words clearly upon our minds. But I think the more likely meaning is that the greatest tonic to the Christian's soul when he is cast down, and one of the strongest incentives to obedience to God, is to appreciate the greatness of God and the glory of Christ. As Christians sing the praise of God and bear in mind one another's needs such praise so successfully turns the soul to God, and to the contemplation of Christ's greatness and glory, that all the soul's ills are dealt with as the complete adequacy of Christ's grace is appreciated afresh.

HOW THE TONIC WORKS

One of the most memorable illustrations of this I've read took place in 1900, when the Boxer uprising in China put the lives of many Christian missionaries in jeopardy. The Revd A.E. Glover and his wife and their two small children, together with a missionary colleague, Miss Gates, had repeated hairbreadth escapes from death. On one occasion, under the pressure of hunger, thirst, and burning heat, Mrs Glover began to show the signs of exhaustion, and there came a moment when she simply lay prostrate, overcome by physical weakness and deeply troubled in soul. In an agony of soul, she cried out from the deep darkness she felt, 'O, God has forsaken us! It can only be that we are not in His will or He would surely never have allowed us to come to this.' Her distress, physically, was such that her husband felt sure she was dying. But that was nothing to the trouble of her soul.

But then something important and significant happened. Scarcely had the words of anguish passed Mrs Glover's lips than God put into Miss Gates' mouth the most wonderful song of praise. Kneeling by the side of her colleague and holding her hand, she poured forth passage after passage, promise after promise, from the Scriptures, exalting the Lord's name, declaring His faithfulness and proving His unchanging and unchangeable love, sworn to us in the everlasting covenant and sealed to us in the blood of His own beloved Son.

Let Archibald Glover continue the story: 'Never shall I forget the music of that heavenly utterance. Instantly the darkness was past and the light was shining again. The expression in my wife's face of joy unspeakable and full of glory, where but a moment before it had been one of unspeakable anguish and distress, was an evident token of what God had wrought. With the tears coursing down her cheeks, she said, "Oh, I will never, never doubt Him again." From that moment her glorious faith never wavered for an instant, but through every future trial only went from strength to strength.

'Then together we repeated right through – with parched lips and stammering tongues, but with hearts that had tasted the wine of heaven – the beautiful hymn, so true to our experience:

> How sweet the name of Jesus sounds
> In a believer's ear!
> It soothes his sorrows, heals his wounds,
> And drives away his fear.

'The effect of this divine cordial upon my dear wife physically, was nothing short of miraculous. From an apparently dying condition she suddenly revived and sat up with a restored vigour which amazed me. By this visitation of God's grace, our hearts were encouraged to wait for His deliverance from a situation which was just as critical as ever.'

These words are really an unconscious testimony to the place of praise in trials.

It is interesting to note that Archibald Glover refers initially to God putting 'into Miss Gates' mouth the most wonderful song of praise.' It would seem to imply that besides using such a lovely hymn as 'How sweet the name of Jesus sounds,' God enabled Miss Gates to express spontaneously praise that was exactly suited to the moment.

In our individual times of worship and of prayer we may find ourselves expressing our praise of God both in spoken word and in song. Sometimes hymns and songs which are already well-known to us will exactly suit our situation. But the Holy Spirit has not exhausted the human language and all the hymns and songs which can be written in praise of God have not yet been written!

I, like many others, have had a regular responsibility in sharing in the leadership of God's people's corporate praise. It is right to try to prepare thoroughly and prayerfully beforehand. But that preparation must not be so rigid that it cannot be altered at the time when God's people come together, if praise in some particular way is prompted by reading of the Word of God, or by some news of God's gracious goodness and intervention on behalf of His people.

There is a place for a variety of praise in our singing. Some of our praise will be what may be described as more 'mindful' in that it concentrates upon many of the glorious truths about God in brief compass. Take, for instance, the hymn we have already mentioned, 'How sweet the name of Jesus sounds', where it gathers titles of the Lord Jesus together:

> Jesus! my Shepherd, Saviour, Friend:
> My Prophet, Priest and King:
> My Lord, my Life, my Way, my End:
> Accept the praise I bring.

Other praise will be more devotional in the sense that we concentrate perhaps on just one aspect of God's revelation and strive to rest in it, as, for instance, when we dwell on God's love in a hymn like 'Loved with everlasting love ...'

Other praise will be more like a love song, as in Psalm 116, when the writer declares, 'I love the LORD, for he heard my voice.'

Some of our praise will be more 'horizontal' in that we talk about God to each other. We sing, 'Come, let us join our cheerful songs ...' or 'Come, let us to the Lord our God with contrite hearts return ...'

Within the context of corporate worship – especially when God's people come together for prayer – there is a place for the blending of individual prayers with corporate singing. But the leading of people in singing must be as spiritual an exercise as leading others in prayer. Those of us who lead others in the offering of praise in song – through the choice of hymns and songs – need to do so thoughtfully and in dependence upon God, for psalms, hymns and spiritual songs have a vital place in God's dealings with His people.

I've known what it is like to go to the church prayer meeting, somewhat weighed down, not feeling much like praying, and perhaps attending out of a sense of duty rather than anticipation of spiritual blessing. And then, suddenly, with the singing of an opening hymn of worship, I've found my thoughts turned away from myself and I've caught a glimpse of the majesty of God and the sufficiency of Christ. The experience has been like the sun shining through the clouds on a dreary day. While God may choose to do this independently of the spirituality of His people's praise, I have the conviction that the more we strive to sing in the Spirit, the more the Lord Jesus Christ will make Himself known, heard and 'seen' through the words of praise that we sing.

PRAISE TO GOD'S NAME

'It is good to praise the LORD and make music to your name, O Most High' (Ps. 92:1) – such words reflect the tenor of Old Testament praise. The Lord Himself is the believer's song (Isa. 12:2). Just as the preoccupation of praise is with God, so too psalms, hymns and spiritual songs are preoccupied with God Himself. The best praise in song centres upon God's self-revelation, and in particular the revelation He has given in the Person and work of His Son. So the more the words of the hymns and songs we sing reflect the words and teaching of Scripture about God and His Son, the more pleasing will our singing be to God, and the more edifying for us.

Attempts have been made to identify evidence of some of the earliest Christian hymns and songs within the New Testament itself. Numerous suggestions have been made, and you will find it helpful to look up the more obvious ones such as Philippians 2:5-11, Colossians 1:15-20, 1 Timothy 3:16 and Revelation 5:12, 19:1, 26. Now if these are indeed quotations from Christian hymns – or if for that matter they became foremost expressions of praise among the early Christians – they all have one significant thing in common: they all focus upon the Person and work of our Lord Jesus Christ.

In worship we submit ourselves to God; we gladly give ourselves to Him in view of His mercy to us in the Lord Jesus (Rom. 12:1). Spiritual singing has a vital part in this and will be at the heart of such worship, for by means of it we express our giving of ourselves to God and our glad submission to His will. The expression of our worship in this way will be encouraged as our submission to God is rekindled and stirred up by the teaching and preaching of God's Word, and by the visual aid the Lord's Supper is of God's mercy to us in our Saviour. Our offering of praise to God by song must never be taken lightly, therefore. It should be entered upon with the deliberate intention of using it to the full for God's ordained purposes.

SINGING GOD'S PRAISE

There are certain principles which should govern our singing of God's praise. First, it should be wholehearted. We are to serve the Lord enthusiastically in whatever we do (Eph. 6:7), our singing included. Half-hearted singing is an offence to God, for He deserves our whole heart, and lethargic singing provides no encouragement to others to sing with their whole heart.

Wholehearted singing is not to be confused with hearty singing. The latter is often thought of as simply loud singing. No doubt some might argue that the two are not completely unrelated! There is a balance to be sought here as elsewhere. To sing wholeheartedly is to match the feelings of our heart with the expression of our lips and, in fact, with our whole being. There are times when we feel like the writer of Psalm 150 who wanted to use every available musical instrument for the praise of God, or the writer of Psalm 47 who wanted the people to clap their hands in their praise of God. Significantly, perhaps, such expressions are not common in the Book of Psalms, and they are not found in the New Testament as the stated norm. But our cultural restraints must not lead us to feel that such expressions are out of place as we sing in our worship of God. It is true, of course, that nothing we do in corporate worship should be a likely hindrance, distraction or stumbling-block to others, but we must not make that rightful caution an excuse for denying all physical and instrumental accompaniments to our worship of God in song.

Secondly, our singing should be intelligent. 'Intelligent' is not to be read as 'intellectual'. 'Intellectual' singing could be thought of as singing which only appeals to the intellect because of the deep doctrine expressed by the words. Certainly there is an important place for what may be described as 'doctrinal' hymns and songs but, as the Book of Psalms itself shows, there is room for great variety in the kind of songs we sing in praise of God. Our singing should engage our intellect, in that our purpose should be to understand what we are singing, and, providing we are in agreement with the words, to take them upon our lips deliberately as our personal praise and prayer to God.

The words we sing should be as careful and as intentional as the prayers we offer to God. We should sing words in the same way that we would express them in ordinary speech, with understanding and emphasis. As important as the sound is the sense. In fact, the sound should echo the sense. The perfection of praise consists in 'all that is within me being stirred up to praise and magnify God.' If the understanding is not employed, and the heart involved, there is no excellence in the music that can ever entitle it to the name of praise. At the same time, appropriate music can assist intelligent, heart-felt praise in its expression.

Thirdly, our singing should be with concentration and spiritual focus. There will always be distractions beckoning us when we worship, sometimes through other members of the congregation, perhaps through people coming in late, or our minds may be full of duties we have left and to which we must return. But our attempt to concentrate as we sing God's praise will not go unrewarded by the Holy Spirit. As we sing, we should focus our attention upon God Himself, and His revelation in His glorious Son, expressing by the way we sing our longing to see His glory and to know deeper fellowship with Him. In the actual moment of praise, unspeakable glimpses of His glory may sometimes be given to our souls, which will cause us to praise Him all the more fervently.

PRIVATE SINGING

Praise in song need not be limited to corporate gatherings of God's people; there is a place for singing in private. I've discovered the helpfulness of a good hymn book. What prompted it in my own case was reading the diary of Jim Elliot, one of the missionaries martyred in an attempt to reach the Auca Indians of Ecuador. He wrote once in his diary, while a student:

'Enjoyed the truth of singing "psalms and hymns and spiritual songs" this morning. Found my prayer list so unstimulating to real prayer that I laid it aside, and took the Inter-Varsity Hymnal and sang aloud with much heart-warming such songs as seemed to fit my need. This is as decidedly a means of grace as anything given by God to His people, but how little we use it!'

On those occasions when, for no accountable reason, it is either difficult to concentrate, or praise and prayer do not flow easily, I pick up my hymn book and sing a hymn of praise. Invariably I find it adds fuel to the embers of my spiritual fervency and I end up rejoicing in the Lord, and wanting to fulfil His purpose for my life – that purpose of being created for His praise.

PRAISE AND MUSIC

Music is assumed to be part of the worship and praise of God to which the Bible summons us. Besides helping us to sing together in harmony, music helps us to remember the words. A good tune assists in meditation as its rhythm expresses the mood and emphasis of the words. Music can express our feelings in a way we find hard to express with our lips. If we think, for example, of Handel's 'Hallelujah Chorus', words and music join together to help us express the praise we know belongs to God alone.

There are problems sometimes in the use of music, however. The difficulties usually arise when it becomes an end in itself, rather than as a means of assisting us to offer our praise in song – when the beauty of the music becomes our focus rather than the beauty of the Lord. Our appreciation of music is, of course, a very personal matter. What is helpful to some is plainly intolerable to others. What some find worshipful others consider a mere jingle! What may be considered to be the more developed tastes of some are frowned upon by others as 'high-brow' and as not at all conducive to worship. Rather than aiming only at a 'mean' which may be neither one thing nor the other, we need to accept both, and be willing to enter into that which is less acceptable to us for the sake of our Christian brother who may find it helpful. In so doing we shall almost certainly find ourselves 'enjoying' it much more than we thought possible, because to behave lovingly and considerately is itself part of our praise of God.

Music should be of the best quality possible, but much more important than musical proficiency are our spiritual longings after God. Something has gone wrong when we are tempted to say, 'Wasn't the music good?' instead of 'How great the Lord is!' That which gives music its place in the worship of God is not its polished perfection – important as the best efforts are in this realm as elsewhere – but in our spiritual longing to honour God and exalt Him by our life and lips.

PRAISE AND DANCE

As Miriam and other women sang the praise of the Lord, they accompanied their praise with tambourines and dancing (Exod. 15:20, 21). Psalms 149 and 150 both contain an exhortation to praise God's Name with dancing (149:3; 150:4). It is important here, as always, to see these exhortations in their context. Dancing in the Old Testament, as it expressed itself in praise of God, was single sex dancing, usually by women. David's dancing is the exception (2 Sam. 6:14, 16). Dance was associated with special victories and was the accompaniment of praise, so that we find women dancing after the crossing of the Red Sea (Exod. 15:20). Dancing after a military victory (1 Sam. 18:6) and at a festival (Judg. 21:19-21) is also mentioned in the Old Testament, but not necessarily in the context of praising God.

There are no references to the use of dance in the New Testament. It has been suggested that this is because the first Christians met in homes where there might be little room to dance, but that seems a weak argument for the New Testament's silence on the subject. Perhaps much more likely is that just as the kiss of love could be abused when given between the sexes, so too can dancing. While some may argue that God can be praised using the language of the body, dancing may encourage a Christian to focus unhelpfully upon the physical, and sexual feelings may be aroused. Admittedly, dancing may do different things to different people, but corporate worship should be as free as possible from anything which is known to be unhelpful. In debateable areas such as dancing, there is a very thin line between what may be helpful and worshipful to some and what may be a merely enjoyable or even lust-provoking sensation to others.

The whole object of praise is to praise God with our spirit and to exercise the soul in its most appropriate occupation. Any activity connected with the praise of God which deflects the soul from its meditation and concentration on God Himself is best abandoned, no matter how innocent it may be in itself and in its proper place. Furthermore, when the people of God join together in praise of God, none should be spectators and all should be participators. While not everyone may enjoy singing, we are more inclined to sing than to dance. Singing is urged upon us in the New Testament (Eph. 5:19, 20; Col. 3:16), whereas dancing is not.

A Prayer

Heavenly Father, I'm so glad that I can sincerely say that it's good to praise You and make music to Your Name, and to proclaim Your love in the morning and Your faithfulness at night. You have made me glad by Your love in the Lord Jesus, and all You have done for me in Him – and what You continue to do day by day. I want to sing for joy at Your goodness.

Help me in my singing to tell of all Your wonderful acts, and to contribute helpfully to the corporate praise of Your people. May I learn how to minister to others in the way in which I sing. To this end, may Your Spirit enable me to sing wholeheartedly, intelligently, and with my focus on You and Your Son, the Lord Jesus.

I want the songs of praise I sing to be the expression of my giving myself afresh to You. I ask this for the sake of Him who gave Himself for me – Jesus Christ, my Lord. Amen.

4

Praise in Prayer

Praise is prayer. When I lift up my heart to God to praise Him, I talk to Him and commune with Him. Prayer is not all asking. As Thomas Watson, the seventeenth-century Puritan, quaintly put it, 'Many have tears in their eyes, and complaints in their mouth, but few have harps in their hand, blessing and glorifying God. Let us honour God this way. Praise is the quit-rent we pay to God: while God renews our lease, we must renew our rent.'

PRAYER ITSELF IS PRAISE

To pray to God is to praise Him. In prayer – even when I am not specifically praising God by spending time thinking about one of His attributes – I am acknowledging God as the One who is supremely worthy of my trust, and uniquely powerful to help me.

Let's imagine that I contract a serious illness. My own doctor declares himself unable to advise or help, but recommends specialists who may be able to assist. After much enquiry and searching, I hear of a leading specialist in the relevant field of medicine and immediately I place myself in his hands. Now, without my uttering any compliments to him, my action constitutes praise of the doctor concerned. My trust in him indicates my assessment of his competence and worth.

Or imagine that I want to go to a concert one evening. I peruse the advertisements and there are a number of concerts from which to choose. I discover, however, that a celebrated violinist is playing, and in choosing to go to his concert rather than the others, I give him a form of unspoken praise.

True prayer is in itself part of our praise of God. We go to Him in a way we go to no one else. He is able to help us as no one else can. His ability surpasses that of all whom we know. Furthermore, in prayer we submit ourselves to God's will – we pray 'Your will be done on earth as it is in heaven' (Matt. 6:10) as the foundation of all our other prayers. By our acknowledgement that God's will is best, we praise God indirectly for His infinite and perfect wisdom.

I remember a father sharing with me, with considerable joy, how his daughter, in her middle twenties, had come into his study one evening and poured out to him her distress over a personal relationship which had gone wrong. His pleasure was not, of course, in his daughter's distress, but in the fact that she felt so assured of his love and concern that she could unburden herself freely and find relief through his understanding. Without saying a word about him, she was nevertheless praising him as a father – she was acknowledging what a good father she knew him to be. When we pour out our hearts to God in prayer, in a way we can do with no one else, we are praising God, we are telling Him what an incomparably good Father we know He is.

AN IMPORTANT INFLUENCE

Praise influences prayer for good. Praise enables us to pray with understanding. John Newton captured the thought well in his hymn, 'Come my soul, thy suit prepare ...' in the verse which reads:

> Thou art coming to a King,
> Large petitions with thee bring:
> For His grace and power are such
> None can ever ask too much.

Praise causes us to look up into God's face. Praise brings before our eyes God's majesty, sovereignty, power and grace, so that we appreciate that whatever we ask or whatever we imagine God can do, He can in fact do far more (Eph. 3:20)!

Praise enables us to grasp that God concerns Himself on the one hand with the little things that may bother us – because He is the God of infinite love and care – but that, on the other hand, He wants us to plead with confidence even for the rulers and nations of the world who are but as dust on the scales in comparison with His might (1 Tim. 2:1-4; Isa. 40:15).

Praise enables us, therefore, to pray with faith. With my eyes upon myself or upon the Church, my expectation of change, progress and advance will be small and petty. But with my eyes upon God and all that He is to me in Jesus Christ, my expectation may know no limits. 'Coming to a King', 'large petitions' are specially appropriate.

Prayer is one wing and faith is the other to lift us heavenward. Try to fly with only one wing! But when faith fixes its gaze upon God, prayer brings us into touch with the limitless resources of our Lord Jesus Christ, and we know that we can do all things as He strengthens us, in answer to our petitions.

PROPER STARTING-POINTS

Praise prompts prayer, or gets prayer started, as it were, something like the choke of a car. I love the account in the Book of Acts of the apostles' reaction when they were commanded not to speak or teach at all in the name of Jesus. They answered, 'We cannot help speaking about what we have seen and heard' (Acts 4:20). Further threats were made to them and they were released. Immediately they went back to their own people and reported all that the chief priests and elders had said to them. Now perhaps the instinctive reaction today, if we were instructed not to preach about Jesus, would be to call a committee meeting or a seminar for consultation among Christian leaders. But the early Christians convened a prayer meeting.

Notice their starting point: 'Sovereign Lord,' they said, 'you made the heaven and the earth and the sea, and everything in them. You spoke by the Holy Spirit through the mouth of your servant, our father David: "Why do the nations rage and the people plot in vain? The kings of earth take their stand and the rulers gather together against the Lord and against his Anointed One"' (Acts 4:24-26).

They began by recalling God's sovereignty and almighty power both in creation and in the affairs of men. In other words, they began not with their immediate situation but with God Himself. But how effectively their praise of God related to their situation! With God on the throne, and His power available to all who honour His Son and do His will, they went on to ask, 'Now, Lord, consider their threats and enable your servants to speak your word with great boldness. Stretch out your hand to heal and perform signs and wonders through the name of your holy servant Jesus' (Acts 4:29, 30). Far from asking God to stop the hindrances, they asked Him to use them to advance His purposes. No wonder Luke is able to record, 'After they prayed, the place where they were meeting was shaken. And they were all filled with the Holy Spirit and spoke the word of God boldly' (31).

God answered their prayers. The unusual but significant proof of this was that 'the place where they were meeting was shaken.' By giving them this sign of His presence (Exod. 19:18; Isa. 6:4; Amos 9:5; Hab. 3:6), God was assuring them that He had heard their prayer (cf. John 12:28-30). This reassurance must have been an inspiring encouragement to this group of early disciples who were experiencing, perhaps for the first time, the full hostility which the preaching of the Lord Jesus as the risen Saviour and Lord can provoke. But their eyes were not so much upon their persecutors but upon the Lord Himself (Acts 4:24f), and their beginning with praise brought about a dynamic experience of God. It was not that they had doubted God's reality, but now they knew His reality afresh. They were sure He was completely involved in that moment of crisis in the life of His people. They had known He could empower them, and now they were filled again with the joy of His salvation. And all because they had begun their prayers with praise – with praise that lifted their eyes away from their immediate problems to God, the unchanging One.

It is not unreasonable to suggest that the timely earthquake that took place some years later, when Paul and Silas were in prison in Philippi, was again a sign that prayer had been heard (Acts 16:25, 26). Significantly, they too had been 'praying and singing hymns to God' (25). While it is not normal for God to give such unusual signs of answering prayer, it is still true that as His people praise Him by making His glory the starting point of their prayers, it is His prerogative to give uncommon signs of His presence when He knows that that is the precise encouragement or deliverance His people need in some seemingly desperate situation.

SEEING THINGS STRAIGHT

Praise also enables us to pray with a proper perspective. I expect many of us have had the experience of becoming extremely upset about a situation and afterwards laughing at ourselves that we allowed it to happen. In my own experience this kind of thing happens when I forget to praise and thank God for His past goodness to me. What happens is that something goes wrong in my life, and I so easily panic. I imagine the worst possible course of events must follow, and all appears black. I then make not only myself miserable but others too. But that situation may be avoided if I begin by pondering God's past dealings with me, and all that He is to me now in Jesus Christ. So instead of saying, 'How on earth am I going to get through this?' I begin by saying to God, 'I thank You for all You have been to me *in the past*, and I praise you *now* that Your grace in Jesus Christ is more than sufficient for this new situation, and I dare to pray that You may be praised by means of it, as I demonstrate what You can mean to an ordinary person like myself.'

Perhaps the word 'thanksgiving' in Philippians 4:6 should be underlined by us: 'Do not be anxious about anything, but in every situation, by prayer and petition, *with thanksgiving*, present your requests to God.' And, significantly, the exhortation is prefaced by another: 'Rejoice in the Lord always. I will say it again: Rejoice!' (4:4). The reminder that no matter how my circumstances change the Lord does not change, and that He has been my constant Deliverer, calls forth renewed praise – whatever my circumstances – and provides a proper perspective as I pray, for I ask Him then with confidence to renew His kindness to me.

When Martin Luther was in the depths of despair his wife took the rather bold and dramatic step of dressing herself in black, so that he asked, 'Who has died?' Her reply was that by his behaviour he gave the impression that God had. This salutary rebuke was sufficient to arouse him to the renewed exercise of faith, and praise to God. God lives! His Son Jesus Christ rose from the dead and is at God's right hand for us. Praise places our needs in the perspective of God's power and grace.

THE PLACE OF SILENCE

Praise in prayer need not always be expressed in words - whether spoken in the heart or by the lips. It may be a prayer too deep for words. There is a place, therefore, for silence in our coming before God. We praise Him when we simply wait silently before Him. 'Be still and know that I am God,' the Lord instructs (Ps. 46:10). 'The Lord is in his holy temple; let all the earth be silent before him,' urges Habakkuk (2:20). Here, as elsewhere, there is 'a time to be silent and a time to speak' (Eccles. 3:7).

Since God hears without words, through silence we may talk to Him. Because God can read our hearts more easily than we can read a book, God hears without our putting our feelings always into words.

We may praise God by silence when we accept His fatherly discipline – no matter how severe. We praise Him when we do not open our mouths in complaint or self-justification, but we keep silent before Him, knowing that He is the one who has dealt with us, and all His dealings with us are just and merciful. Or we may say a few words of worshipping submission and then remain silent, as did Job, after he had said, 'The LORD gave and the LORD has taken away; may the name of the LORD be praised' (Job 1:21).

There are other times when silent prayer is especially appropriate. If, for example, we know something of God causing all His goodness to be brought home to us, the appropriate response will be in the worship of hearts that are silent as they are lost in wonder, love and praise. One night George Whitefield, the great eighteenth-century evangelist, preached with such power and evidences of God working in people's lives, that he could scarcely speak any more because of his sense of awe. 'After I came home,' he wrote in his journal, 'I threw myself upon the bed, and in awful silence admired the infinite freedom, sovereignty, and condescension of the love of God.' Silence provides the soul with scope and opportunity to ponder God's greatness.

To be able to sit in silence and enjoy another person's company is a mark of deep and true friendship. A love which has no silence sometimes has no depth in it. Observe, for example, a loving mother watching her children as they romp and play close by. Or watch a young man who has just become engaged, looking at his fiancée as she comes into the room. Their eyes – and their silence – may say more than their words.

Silence has another importance: there are things we do not hear unless we are silent. Where I live we can sometimes hear the fog-horns on the vessels that go up and down the Firth of Forth. But we hear them usually first thing in the morning and late at night. It is not that they sound only then, but that we are only quiet then. Most of us live with what often can be the nuisance of noise. In moments of silent prayer, when by the attitude of our heart we express our praise of God, we may find Him working in our lives, and enabling us to discern His voice in ways we would otherwise miss.

A weaned child gives unspoken praise to its mother as it rests content and satisfied in her arms. David wrote, 'I have stilled and quieted my soul; like a weaned child with its mother, like a weaned child is my soul within me' (Ps. 131:2). As we cause our souls to dwell upon Him whom we love we shall find ourselves not only silent in adoring worship, but we shall find them still and quiet, satisfied with His superlative goodness. We praise God by relaxing in His presence as our heavenly Father who accepts us because we are His sons and daughters by a wonderful act of adoption.

EXAMPLES OF PRAISE IN PRAYER

Hannah – the mother of Samuel – expresses in prayer her appreciation of God (1 Sam. 2:1-10). Her heart 'rejoices in the LORD' (1) and she delights in acknowledging God's uniqueness: 'There is no one holy like the LORD; there is no one besides you; there is no Rock like our God' (2). It is a prayer we can profitably use when we ourselves find the offering of praise difficult. There would seem to be little doubt that others throughout the ages, like Mary (cf. Luke 1:46-55), have been helped by its example.

The Lord's Prayer provides a further illustration. Its first preoccupation is the Name of the Lord. 'Our Father in heaven, hallowed be your name' (Matt. 6:9). To hallow God's Name is to reverence His Name; and those who reverence God's Name praise Him for all that He is in Himself. When we pray the first petition of the Lord's Prayer we are asking, in effect, that we and all men may fulfil God's purpose for us in that we are created to praise Him. While the words, 'Yours is the kingdom and the power and the glory for ever' (13) do not appear in the earlier manuscripts, they do express the legitimate convictions that prayer should both begin and end with praise of God.

The apostle Paul nowhere provides an exposition of the place of praise in prayer, but his letters indicate the pre-eminent position he gave to it. Think, for example, of his doxologies: 'Oh, the depth of the riches of the wisdom and knowledge of God! How unsearchable his judgements, and his paths beyond tracing out! "Who has known the mind of the Lord? Or who has been his counsellor?" "Who has ever given to God, that God should repay them?" For from him and through him and for him are all things. To him be the glory for ever! Amen' (Rom. 11:33-36).

Again, 'Now to him who is able to do immeasurably more than all we ask or imagine, according to his power that is at work within us, to him be glory in the church and in Christ Jesus throughout all generations, for ever and ever! Amen' (Eph. 3:20, 21). Spontaneously he bursts out into praise as he writes: 'Praise be to the God and Father of our Lord Jesus Christ, who has blessed us in the heavenly realms with every spiritual blessing in Christ' (Eph. 1:3); and again, 'Praise be to the God and Father of our Lord Jesus Christ, the Father of compassion and the God of all comfort, who comforts us in all our troubles ... ' (2 Cor. 1:3, 4). Paul's prayers constantly overflow into thanksgiving. 'Thanks be to God!' is his cry (Rom. 6:17; 7:25; 2 Cor. 2:14) and 'I thank my God every time I remember you ...' is his assurance to readers of his letters (Phil. 1:3; Col. 1:3; 1 Thess. 1:2; 2 Thess 1:3; Philem. 4).

USE THE CHOKE

Perhaps we need to pull out the 'spiritual choke' of praise in prayer much more than we do. Certainly that's true for myself. If we compile our list of God's attributes in our prayer diary, with helpful Scriptures placed against each, this will certainly assist us. Equally helpful – and sometimes even more stimulating – is to read the Scriptures with the deliberate endeavour to lay hold of truths they teach about God Himself, and for which we can praise Him.

The best way for me to illustrate this method is perhaps not to choose obvious passages but two passages I have read today in the course of my daily reading. The first was Psalm 93, and as I read it in the New International Version (1984) I noted words and phrases which speak of God himself: 'The LORD reigns, he is robed in majesty ... armed with strength ... Your throne was established long ago; you are from all eternity ... the LORD on high is mighty ... holiness adorns your house for endless days ... (1, 2, 4, 5). Notice how many attributes of God just tumble out, one after another in this one psalm: God's sovereignty, majesty, strength, eternity, might and holiness. My heart soon responded as I meditated upon these features of God's character, and I found myself responding in praise. Praise then moved to prayer as I asked God for strength for today, and God's might to achieve holiness in my life.

The other passage, totally different, was Acts 16:6-34, which begins with Paul's vision of the man of Macedonia, his arrival with Silas, and perhaps others, in Philippi, and the conversion of Lydia and the Philippian jailer – the latter after Paul and Silas were thrown into prison unjustly for being instrumental in delivering a slave girl from an evil spirit. It was not difficult to look at the passage from the point of view of God's attributes, and with the desire to praise Him. First, God's power to guide His servants stands out (6-12). Second, God's grace in opening a woman's heart to respond to Paul's message (14). Third, God's power to deliver men and women from Satan (18), and His servants from prison (26). And fourth, God's saving grace in our Lord Jesus Christ so freely extended to all who believe (30-34). Once again the offering of praise prompted prayer: prayer for guidance, the opening of people's hearts to the gospel, the salvation of men and women from Satan's power, the deliverance of God's servants in prison and the conversion of whole families.

If we begin by praising God in our prayers there is little doubt that we shall end up as we ought. We both pray correctly and end by praising Him all the more. To this end we were created.

A Prayer

Forgive me, Lord, that often my prayers have been nearly all asking, with too little praising and thanking You. And yet I thank You too that my praying – even when full of so many requests – is praise of You because You are the only One to whom I can turn, and I can be absolutely sure of Your faithfulness and steadfast love.

But I do want to praise You as I ought in my prayers. Help me to fix my eyes upon You, and all that You have become to me in Jesus Christ, and to make Your glory the starting-point of my prayers, so that my expectancy may know no limits.

Teach me to know the time when it is right to be silent before You, and when it is time to speak. May I not miss anything You want to say to me through my eagerness to speak without listening.

Help me to come into Your presence with that paradoxical mixture of awe and joy – awe, because of Your greatness, and joy as I relax in Your presence because You enable me by Your Spirit to call You 'Abba, Father'.

Open my eyes daily, as I read Your Word, to lay hold of the truth about Yourself so that I may praise You more and more. I ask for these blessings in the name of Your Son, Jesus Christ.

Amen.

5

Praise in Trials

'Consider it pure joy, my brothers, whenever you face trials of many kinds,' urges James, 'because you know that the testing of your faith produces perseverance' (James 1:2, 3). It is much easier to talk about praise in trials when our life is free of them for a time than when we are in the thick of difficulty and testing. But James was not exaggerating: there is a place for pure joy, for praise of God in trials.

NO ESCAPE

If we would escape trials we must leave this world altogether. Besides being the common lot of mankind, Christian believers sometimes know particular trials on account of their allegiance to the Lord Jesus Christ. 'In this world you will have trouble,' our Lord fore-warned His disciples (John 16:33).

Trials may come through physical suffering. Some have to endure this trial throughout their whole life, others only occasionally, and others perhaps only towards the end of their life. A mystery exists about human suffering which we cannot fathom and it poses many questions which we cannot yet answer, but which will be completely answered in the life to come when we know God fully, even as we are now fully known by Him (1 Cor. 13:12).

There is always a danger of glibness in talking about suffering when we ourselves are not going through it. Suffering tests the reality of faith more than most trials. Nevertheless some of God's most honoured and used sons and daughters have endured the trial of severe suffering, and our Lord Himself knew it to the full.

Trials may come through disappointments. Of course, disappointments can be our own fault, when, for example, we set our sights too high for our ambitions or when we expect too much of other people. But disappointments meet us too through no fault of our own. Broken engagements bring heartbreak, and spoiled relationships may leave inner scars. The hopes we have for the progress of God's work or for the success of our children may fall to the ground, and besides becoming disheartened, we may be secretly demoralised and afraid to share our feelings with others in case we depress them too.

Trials may come through difficulties and temptations. Daily work, marred as it is by the Fall of man, contains an inescapable element of drudgery and routine for most people, and either environment or the attitudes of others can create tensions and unhappiness. The temptations of Satan, our great and subtle enemy, will assault us, and we will find our indwelling corruption a great trial, causing us to cry out, 'What a wretched man I am! Who will rescue me from this body that is subject to death?' (Rom. 7:24).

Opposition and even persecution will be the experience of some Christians in the world, although we must beware of provoking such reactions by thoughtless or unrighteous conduct. There is merit in persecution only if it is genuinely for Christ's sake. If we have parents or brothers and sisters who are antagonistic to our profession of faith in Christ, it will be no small trial sometimes to live peaceably and to persevere in striving to maintain a good relationship with them.

Trials come to all of us eventually through bereavement. Human relationships of love and trust constitute our most valuable possessions. To lose them may leave us utterly desolate. The loneliness a bereaved husband or wife knows does not necessarily grow less as the years pass; it may even increase. And until we experience bereavement, we cannot really appreciate it, much as we try.

The Bible gives us no encouragement to think that we shall be relieved or excused from trials in this life. God does not choose to see His children through their earthly life tucked away in the warmth, luxury and security of a four-star hotel. Rather He sends them out in all weathers on His 'assault course' to realise their faith's potential.

THE IMPORTANT 'BUT'

But we are created to praise – and we are created to praise God in trials as out of them. But it is not easy to praise in trials; and it is certainly not natural to us. The Book of Psalms reveals the struggles – and often the secret conflicts – of men who have found trials so thoroughly immersing them that joy in God for the time being has gone, and so has the ability to praise. 'Why are you downcast, O my soul? Why so disturbed within me?' So the psalmist wrestles with his problem. 'Put your hope in God,' he says to himself, 'for I will yet praise him, my Saviour and my God' (Ps. 42:11; 43:5).

These two psalms underline the fact that part of our praise in trials is simply telling God 'how it is' with us. By pouring out our soul's distress to Him – as we can with no one else – we are declaring how good and faithful we know He is both in understanding us, and caring about how we feel.

Paul found himself in a position of torment through 'a thorn' in his flesh – clearly some physical trial of a distressing nature. Satan made such use of it to try to drag Paul down and discourage him that Paul calls this 'thorn' 'a messenger of Satan' (2 Cor. 12:7). Three times Paul pleaded with the Lord to take it away from him. But the Lord's answer was a plain 'No', and in wrestling with the problem Paul found the Lord's answer and promise of grace. But he did not find that answer all at once, and not without much anguish of soul and heart-searching (2 Cor. 12:9, 10).

Paul learned to praise God by his *happy* submission to God in this particular trial, as in others. Instead of allowing the 'thorn' to become a source of secret bitterness – as well it might have done – it became a means to his praising God as Paul acknowledged that God knew what was best for him. He learned even to boast all the more gladly about his weaknesses, so that Christ's power might rest upon him (2 Cor. 12:9).

How then can we learn to praise God in trials too? And let's be in no doubt about it that such ability is a powerful aspect of Christian testimony in the world. There's no slick answer – and we are rightly suspicious of such answers anyway. The clue is found in the two psalms we have quoted – Psalms 42 and 43. Like the psalmist we may have to argue ourselves into praise. There is a distinct place for talking to ourselves – not in public, of course, but in private. We may properly argue ourselves into praise of God in trials by turning our thoughts to God, in certain deliberate ways, which I'll try to describe in a moment.

PSALM 34

Perhaps an outstanding example of praise in trials is Psalm 34 – a psalm well worth committing to memory. David begins by expressing his determination to praise God always: 'I will extol the LORD at all times; his praise will always be on my lips' (1). Now if we look through the psalm we find David honestly mentioning both his fears (4) and his troubles (6), and he refers to the trials which come through affliction (2), enemies (7), and self-despair (18). Now what was his secret? The answer seems to lie in the two verbs *look* and *call*. 'Those who *look* to him are radiant; their faces are never covered with shame. This poor man *called*, and the LORD heard him; he saved him out of all his troubles' (5, 6). In fact, both these verbs are summed up in the one verb *seek* in verse 4: 'I *sought* the LORD, and he answered me; he delivered me from all my fears.' As David's trials came he learned, and certainly not without difficulty, to turn the eyes of his soul towards the Lord Himself, and as he did so he found prayer flowing from his lips leading into praise of God.

ARGUING OURSELVES INTO PRAISE

What then must we say to ourselves in times of trial so that we praise God as we ought, and sooner rather than later? First, I must say to myself, *'God has not changed.'* Now that is a most obvious thing to say, but my face and my feelings may not be saying it. Trials and difficulties usually indicate some change in our circumstances, and perhaps the threat of ominous changes ahead. Illness may jeopardise our job, or our promotion prospects. Disappointment may bring our plans to nothing. Bereavement alters the whole pattern of our life. *But* God is the same. We may say with David, 'Taste and see that the LORD is good; blessed is the man who takes refuge in him' (Ps. 34:8). God's love is steadfast and He is never a disappointment. 'Jesus Christ is the same yesterday and today and for ever' (Heb. 13:8). Jesus lives!

Secondly, I must say to myself, *'Forget not all his benefits'* (Ps. 103:2). While trials indicate that some areas of our life are black, not everything is black. For example, I find it a severe trial to be away from my wife and family for any long time. If I am not careful the experience of separation depresses me, and I can lose my joy. But if I remember His benefits I begin by recalling His goodness in giving me, in the first place, a family whom I miss so much, and who love me as I love them. So instead of complaining, I thank Him!

When work overwhelms me because of its seemingly ceaseless pressures I can go about it grudgingly, finding the whole daily routine a hard trial. But if I remember God's benefits, I thank Him that I am employed, that I know that He has provided me with my daily occupation, and that I can please Him through the work I do. And so I praise Him. With the identical pile of letters on my desk and the same number of people to see or visit, I even sing as I go about my work. The difficulties and workload have not changed, but my way of looking at them has.

An unfortunate myth circulates to the effect that all work should be fulfilling and creative. But such a view is devoid of realism, and certainly so in a fallen world. Some jobs, especially on a factory floor or in an office, are essentially repetitive and uncreative. Of course, it is not wrong to seek a job which is exactly suited to our temperament, but we must not regard it as a disaster if we do not find it. Ever since the Fall of man there has been an element of futility about man's work (Gen. 3:17-19), and it is only when our relationship to God is right through our Lord Jesus Christ that the element of futility is brought under control and rectified, though we still have to undertake perhaps monotonous and repetitious employment. Even in the most humdrum jobs we can praise God that our work is a means of answering our prayer of 'Give us today our daily bread.' We can praise Him too that in all probability our leisure time will mean more to us than many others because we appreciate the opportunity of expressing our creativity in hobbies or do-it-yourself activities of our own choice. What is more, by our wages, honourably earned, we may 'have something to share with those in need' (Eph. 4:28).

Thirdly, I must say to myself, '*Remember God's promises.*' God's promises are the currency of faith in that, just as I use the money in my pocket or the notes in my wallet to deal with the financial demands of the day, so I should use God's promises to deal with the spiritual demands – or trials – of the day. The delightful thing is that they never run out with using as ordinary currency may. As we think of trials in general relevant promises tumble out of the Bible's pages. 'We know,' Paul assures us, 'that in all things God works for the good of those who love him, who have been called according to his purpose' (Rom. 8:28). In the same chapter he asks the question, 'Who shall separate us from the love of Christ?' and he provides a sample catalogue of human trials: 'Shall trouble or hardship or persecution or famine or nakedness or danger or sword?' (35). 'No,' he declares, 'in all these things we are more than conquerors through him who loved us.' (37). There is great strength in the little word 'in'. It is not out of difficulties that God makes us more than conquerors but in them – a different matter altogether. Paul's climax is reached with the words: 'For I am convinced that neither death nor life, neither angels nor demons, neither the present nor the future, nor any powers, neither height nor depth, nor anything else in all creation, will be able to separate us from the love of God that is in Christ Jesus our Lord' (38, 39). In view of the anxiety our trials bring about in our life now and in the days to come, those words 'neither the present nor the future' bring particular reassurance.

We have other promises too, such as 1 Corinthians 10:13: 'No temptation has overtaken you except what is common to mankind. And God is faithful; he will not let you be tempted beyond what you can bear. But when you are tempted, he will also provide a way out so that you can stand up under it.' Sometimes a promise itself may provide that 'way out' in that it brings before us the assurance of God's love and care for us in our trials, and we turn to Him in praise. How can we not praise God in our trials when, fixing our mind on His promises, we remember that 'no matter how many promises God has made, they are "Yes" in Christ' (2 Cor. 1:20). Trials may drive us to God's promises as little else may do – and always to our profit and to the praise of God in our lives.

Fourthly, I must say to myself, '*Look for God's purpose in the trials.*' If James' words, 'Consider it pure joy, my brothers, whenever you face trials of many kinds,' (1:2), stood on their own, I think they would represent a ridiculous and harmful approach to life. In fact, I would be mentally ill to adopt such an approach. But James' counsel does not stop there. He provides the grounds of his exhortation: 'because you know that the testing of your faith produces perseverance. Let perseverance finish its work so that you may be mature and complete, not lacking anything' (1:3, 4). There are some aspects of the fruit of the Spirit which can be produced only by 'pruning' or 'testing'. It is possible to emerge from testing a far better Christian and a more useful servant of God. While in 'the furnace' of his trials, Job exclaims, 'But he knows the way that I take; when he has tested me, I shall come forth as gold' (Job 23:10). Sometimes I pray, 'Lord, I want to be my best for You. Fashion me according to Your will so that I please You in all I do.' By testings and trials God may often take me at my word. God always has some reward awaiting us at the conclusion of our trials (James 1:12). Trials are frequently a preparation for blessing. Our difficulties provide stepping stones for the feet of our faith, and they lead to stronger faith and increased Christlikeness of character. When we talk to ourselves in the light of this understanding – together with the knowledge that 'the Lord disciplines the one he loves' (Heb. 12:6) – we stop moaning, complaining and being sorry for ourselves and instead we praise God for the privilege He entrusts to us with our trials. We praise Him for His patience with us, and the confidence He reposes in us. Samuel Rutherford, a godly seventeenth-century pastor and teacher, had to suffer much for his witness to his Saviour, even being sent to prison. He came to recognise that the Lord Jesus, in His mercy, makes room for Himself in our lives by our losses. A thought worth pondering. And George Whitefield found that trials made the prospect of heaven doubly agreeable. When the Lord Jesus becomes more precious to us, and heaven increasingly attractive, we praise God – not out of our trials but in them!

Finally, I must say to myself, 'Remember God's dealings with others in the past.' While Hebrews 11 illustrates the power of faith in the lives of the spiritual giants of the Old Testament, practically every illustration relates to faith tested by trials. More, for example, is said about Abraham than anyone else (8-19) and none was tested more than he was. Testing is one of the means by which God carries forward His saving purposes. The person concerned does not always know until afterwards whether or not, or why, God has been testing him. But his gratitude is great when he is enabled to come out of difficulty strong in faith, not only preserved and proved, but purified, disciplined, strengthened and taught. Abraham stands out as an example of a man kept through great testing.

As Richard Keen puts it,

> When through fiery trials thy pathway shall lie,
> His grace all-sufficient shall be thy supply;
> The flame shall not hurt thee, His only design
> Thy dross to consume and thy gold to refine.

An unseen spiritual contest was the background to Job's trials. Disaster upon disaster fell upon him: he lost his farm animals (1:13-15), his flocks (16), his camels

(17), together with many of his servants, and, finally his children (18, 19). His response, quite remarkably, was one of worship and praise: 'Naked I came from my mother's womb, and naked I will depart. The LORD gave and the LORD has taken away; may the name of the LORD be praised.' (21). However, the remarkable conclusion of the book is: 'The LORD blessed the latter part of Job's life more than the former part' (42:12). James takes this example up, in the context of trials, and urges, 'You have heard of Job's perseverance and have seen what the Lord finally brought about. The Lord is full of compassion and mercy' (James 5:11). Before we are permitted to see what the Lord will finally bring out of our trials, we may praise Him for He will not fail us – His compassion and mercy, guaranteed to us in Christ, are everlasting.

However, the message of Job 1:21 to us is to praise God because He is God, in all circumstances, and not simply because, as in Job's case, God's purpose was to restore Job's wealth.

'A Christian, as a child of God, must always rejoice, always sing, fear nothing, always be free from care, and always glory in God,' Luther wrote. When we are slow to reason with ourselves in our times of difficulty, we fail to praise God as we ought. But perhaps God's dealings with others in the past may help us here too. I've wondered if it is significant that it was about midnight when Paul and Silas were praying and singing hymns to God in the inner cell of the prison at Philippi (Acts 16:25). Understandably, their first reaction may have been one of despair and depression. Their backs were bleeding, and the small company of believers at Philippi were being denied the benefits of the ministry of the missionaries whom God had used to bring them to Christ. But could it be that Paul and Silas 'came to themselves', and perhaps helped one another to praise God?

Perhaps Paul said to Silas, 'Don't let's forget that God brought us so clearly to Philippi in the first place.' 'Yes,' Silas probably responded, 'and the Lord has promised to be with us, and He must have some good purpose in permitting this trial to occur.' 'Amen to that,' maybe Paul replied. 'Think of all of God's promises assuring us of deliverance and of the certainty of His sovereign purposes. Let's pray together.' And as they sought the Lord, looking to Him and calling upon Him, they were made radiant, and they sang hymns to God at midnight. It is better to come round to singing praise even as late as midnight when we are in trials than not to do so at all.

The secret of praise in trials is stirring ourselves up to look consciously at the Lord and soon, if not always immediately, we shall be saying, 'I will praise the LORD, who counsels me, even at night my heart instructs me. I have set the LORD always before me. Because he is at my right hand, I will not be shaken' (Ps. 16:7, 8).

Sometimes, perhaps like Paul and Silas in prison, we may minister to one another when we sense that a fellow-believer, on account of his trials, has lost his practice of praise. Just as one live coal adds warmth and fire to a dying coal, so one believer, gently and genuinely saying, 'Glorify the LORD with me; let us exalt his name together' (Ps. 34:3), may bring the desire to praise God to another believer's soul.

What so often happens is that as in time of trial we deliberately praise God as we ought, we find ourselves calling to Him for help, and then we find that His deliverance from the trial comes. Perhaps this is what David meant when he declared: 'I called to the LORD, who is worthy of praise, and have been saved from my enemies' (2 Sam. 22:4).

A PRAYER

Lord, forgive me when I've been glib in my talking about trials, especially when mine have been small and few.

Forgive me when I've asked You to fashion me according to Your will, and then I've been surprised at the testings and trials You have either sent or permitted in my life as part of Your answer to my prayers.

Forgive me too when I've failed to submit to Your directing or chastening hand on my life, and I've allowed bitterness to take root in my heart.

I want to tell You now that I love You. I praise You that it is because You love me that You discipline me. I thank You too that You discipline me always for my good, so that I may share in Your holiness.

I praise You that in all that happens to me at this present time. You are working things together for good, whether I see it to be so in this life or I have to wait until the next. When greater trials come, help me to remember how I've prayed now, and to renew my joyful submission to Your fatherly control of my life. I ask this in the Name of my Saviour who Himself learned obedience from what He suffered, and who lived to praise You.

Amen.

6

Praise in Everyday Life

'I will extol the LORD at all times; his praise will always be on my lips.' These opening words of Psalm 34 are rather special to me through a particular circumstance. I was afforded a delightful opportunity of visiting India. Because I knew I would be speaking at meetings day after day, I determined that I would take Psalm 34 and meditate upon it, a verse each day for the good of my own soul, quite independently of the passages from which I would be preaching.

Beginning my journey in Edinburgh, I had to break my journey in London to catch a plan from Heathrow the next morning. As I got undressed that night I discovered that I had developed a rather unpleasant skin rash which affected particularly my arms. Most of the shirts my wife had packed in my suitcase were short-sleeved, in keeping with the warmth of the Indian climate. I realised that wearing them with this skin rash was going to be difficult, if not impossible. As I picked up my Bible and read Psalm 34, the first verse for my meditation was 'I will extol the LORD at all times; his praise will always be on my lips.' And so I praised Him.

Throughout the month I was in India, I had to wear my long-sleeved shirts, and the first words of Psalm 34 were a necessary and helpful reminder to me not to be preoccupied with myself – and my petty irritation – but with God Himself. Words can hardly convey the spiritual blessing this small thing became.

When we rightly affirm that we are created to praise God we are implying that praise, happily, does not have to be limited to expressions of praise in song or speech, but that the life we live can be praise. The writer to the Hebrews links the two together when he urges, 'Through Jesus, therefore, let us continually offer to God a sacrifice of praise – the fruit of lips that confess his name. And do not forget to do good and to share with others, for with such sacrifices God is pleased' (13:15, 16).

Praise in everyday life is rightly assumed by the writer to the Hebrews to be a thrilling, enjoyable and stimulating experience. He acknowledges that his Christian readers are going through difficulty and sometimes persecution, but he does not want them to shirk the reality of the Cross in everyday life. To stimulate them to praise, he reminds them of their unchanging Saviour (13:8), His saving work on their behalf, and of the wonderful future to which they looked forward (13:10-14). These truths underline the force of the word '*therefore*', and that it is '*through Jesus*' that we can praise God continually.

To praise God when we are in difficulties – and not least when some of the difficulties arise from our faithfulness to Him (cf. Acts 5: 41; 16:16-25) – may cost us something, but that only enhances our 'sacrifice of praise'. We have joy then in identifying with David who declared, 'I will not sacrifice to the LORD my God burnt offerings that cost me nothing.' (2 Sam. 24:24). Of course, we are not to go around searching for difficulties as if some merit were to be gained by them. But when they come in the ordinary course of events we enhance our praise of God as we accept them submissively as from the hand of our Father in heaven. Our praise of God is probably at its best in daily life when we trust Him in defiance of the pressures not to.

It is worth noting too that the offering of praise when hardship, illness or other trials come is often the first stage in discovering God's deliverance or healing. All the time we are lacking in praise, we fail to exercise faith. But as we exercise faith in God by praising Him, we may find Him doing the most surprising things for us (cf. Acts 16:25, 26). 'He who sacrifices thank-offerings honours me,' declares the Lord, 'and he prepares the way *so that I may show him the salvation of God*' (Ps. 50:23; cf 12-15). The path we deliberately tread as we praise God in difficulty so often becomes the path God uses to send His blessings along.

We should not overlook too in Hebrews 13:15 the word *continually*. 'Through Jesus, therefore, let us *continually* offer to God a sacrifice of praise ...' It is the identical word Paul used when he said, 'I strive *always* to keep my conscience clear before God and man' (Acts 24:16). While praise cannot be a continual activity of our lips, it can be the continual attitude of our mind. The whole of life can be an act of praise to God as the Lord Jesus is acknowledged in attitudes, as well as in speech and actions.

Horatius Bonar wrote a hymn which includes the following two verses:

Not for the lip of praise alone,
Nor e'en the praising heart
I ask, but for a life made up
Of praise in every part.

Praise in the common things of life,
Its goings out and in;
Praise in each duty and each deed,
However small and mean.

One of George Herbert's hymns begins with the verse:

Teach me, my God and King
In all things Thee to see,
And what I do in anything
To do it as for Thee.

The convictions expressed in these two hymns find support in Paul's exhortations: 'And whatever you do, whether in word or deed, do it all in the name of the Lord Jesus, giving thanks to God the Father through him ... Whatever you do, work at it with all your heart, as working for the Lord, not for human masters ... So whether you eat or drink or whatever you do, do it all for the glory of God' (Col. 3:17, 23; 1 Cor. 10:31).

Glibness is always an enemy of reality, and we know how easy it is for phrases like 'to the glory of God' to trip off our tongues without our really understanding in practical terms what we mean. We need to wrestle with this question, therefore, of how our life may be genuinely lived to God's praise.

Life is made up of many humdrum tasks and not a few irksome duties. What of the harassed young mother with the continual demands of her children? Can she live her life continually praising God? And what of the husband, with the pressures of keeping on top of his work and providing security for his family? Can he live and work in his office or on his shop floor to God's praise? And what of the person who has to repeat the same action time after time in a factory? Can he or she praise God in the course of daily work? The answer is 'Yes'!

THANKFULNESS

We praise God in everyday life as we live *thankfully*. 'Give thanks in all circumstances,' is the apostolic injunction, for together with other things, 'this is God's will for you in Christ Jesus' (1 Thess. 5:18). The emphasis must be upon the 'all circumstances'. Of course, the harassed young mother can go through the day bemoaning the work she has to do – the nappies to change, clothes to wash and iron, the meals to prepare, the washing up afterwards. But, on the other hand, she can thank God for the gift of her children – for God has given them to her and her husband – and the privileges of bringing them up in a way that will make it easy for them to appreciate God's love in the Lord Jesus, and find their lives fulfilled in His service in the years to come. The husband at work or the person at the factory bench can be kicking against the irritations and frustrations of daily employment, living for the weekends rather than for the present moment. But, on the other hand, they can thank God that they have employment when others do not, and that by their work they provide for their families.

When we live thankfully, we praise God. Inevitably, times will come when people say, 'How can you be so cheerful?' and the answer, simply and sincerely, will be, 'Well, I have so much for which to thank God.' It is not our circumstances which need to change so very often, but our attitude to them. When I live thankfully – whatever my lot – I praise God, for I am silently declaring that I believe God knows what is best for me, and I count His will as best.

WHOLEHEARTEDNESS

We praise God in everyday life as we live and work *wholeheartedly*. 'Whatever you do, work at it with all your heart, as working for the Lord, not for men' (Col. 3:23). The impressiveness of these words increases when we appreciate that they were first directed to Christian slaves. How hard it must have been to do an honest day's work when perhaps your master beat you mercilessly or criticised the best of which you were capable! But the slave who cleaned out the stables with a desire to do it as if it were for the Lord Jesus Himself as his true Master had found an effective way of praising the Lord Jesus. The job itself was lifted to a higher level, and over a period of time his earthly master was bound to enquire what made the slave work so conscientiously, and the answer he would receive would bring praise to the name of the Lord Jesus. 'Buy a Christian slave, if you can,' might be the master's advice to another slave-owner.

Whether our work is that of a road-sweeper or the managing director of a group of chain-stores, the wholeheartedness with which we do our proper work is a means of praise to God, and way of drawing attention to the difference He makes to our lives. One evening, taking our dog out for a walk, I met a neighbour who had executive responsibility for the appointment of staff within a large organisation in Edinburgh. He stopped me, and asked, 'Does Mr ... belong to your church fellowship?' To be honest, I was immediately cautious and almost on the defensive. So often, unfortunately, people may be critical of Christian witness, and the person mentioned was a man in his fifties who had only recently been converted. His way of life immediately before his conversion had been very clearly wrong and faith in the Lord Jesus had brought dramatic and wonderful changes in his life. 'Yes,' I replied, perhaps a little cautiously. 'Well,' continued my neighbour, 'he works for us now. If ever you get wind of the fact that he is unsettled because he has had to start from the bottom, please let me know. We want to keep him – he's one of the best employees we've got!' How glad I was to be able to explain what made the difference. Without realising it, my friend had been living to God's praise. Everything we do becomes worthwhile when it can be done with an eye to God's approval, and when our wholeheartedness bears testimony to the fact that God's approval matters most.

HOLINESS

We praise God in our everyday life as we live our lives *holily*. Holiness scarcely figures in the world's vocabulary, and so it tends to be absent from the Christian's too. But it is an irreplaceable word and concept. Loud and clear comes the New Testament's reiteration of the Old Testament's revelation of God's will for His people if they are to live to His praise: 'Be holy, because I am holy' (1 Pet. 1:16). While God's holiness is an awesome thing for sinful men and women to appreciate, it is part of His beauty. When we declare God to be holy we are affirming that He is on the side of all that is noble, right, pure, lovely, admirable, excellent and praiseworthy (cf. Phil. 4:8), and – at the same time – that He is quite apart from all that is sinful and evil.

Perhaps one of the tragedies of the Church's witness – or lack of witness – in the world is that people are given a negative impression of holiness rather than a positive. Now I admit that the god of this world, Satan, does his best to mar Christians' testimony in the eyes of unbelievers, but all the blame cannot be placed on him. Holiness is attractive because it is the reflection of God's character in us. In practice, it means that we are reliable and honest at work, faithful and caring at home, and positive in our contribution to the lives of others. It will also mean that we separate ourselves from evil, whether in terms of favouritism at work or dishonesty, or in terms of immorality and loose talk.

The way to holiness is basically simple for the Christian, indwelt as he is by the Holy Spirit. It is daily obedience to the will of God as he is guided by the Scriptures and the Holy Spirit's application to his conscience of what he knows to be God's will. Obedience itself is perhaps our chief tribute of praise to our holy Father and the Lord Jesus, our holy Saviour, for by it we affirm, 'Your way is right, good and the best!' Every time I take a step of obedience I praise the Father, the Son and the Holy Spirit. The more we draw attention to God's holiness by the lives we live, the more we live to His praise.

CHRISTLIKENESS

Christlikeness is another way of looking at holiness. Our everyday life praises God as we live it with Christlikeness in view. I wonder if you have ever had an outstanding teacher who left his or her mark upon you for good? He taught

84

you things which you have never forgotten, and whenever you are involved in certain situations you remember what he said, or did himself, and you do the same. Now, almost unconsciously you praise your teacher by the correspondence of your own actions with his. We likewise live to God's praise as our manner of life increasingly corresponds with the pattern our Saviour left us to follow.

An unknown writer has expressed what was true of one Christian and what can be true of us all:

> Not only in the words you say
> Nor in the deeds expressed,
> But in the most unconscious way,
> Is Christ by you confessed.

Paul frequently demonstrates how the Lord Jesus Christ sanctifies everyday human experience. At Philippi there was a problem of disunity through bad relation-ships within the church which threatened the church's witness. At the heart of the disunity there may have been the disagreement of two women, Euodia and Syntyche, with perhaps people taking sides. Rather than simply giving in to the situation as a disaster, Paul sees it as an opportunity to demonstrate Christ's penetration of the most difficult situations so that God is praised as His deliverance is experienced afresh. Paul urges all the believers at Philippi to let their attitude be the same as that of our Lord Jesus, and we have the memorable words of Philippians 2:5ff, beginning, 'Your attitude should be the same as that of Christ Jesus: who, being in very nature God, did not consider equality with God something to be grasped ...'

At Corinth the believers needed to be encouraged in a proper stewardship of the money and resources God had given them, and Paul once again shows the relevance of the supreme example of giving: 'For you know the grace of our Lord Jesus Christ, that though he was rich, yet for your sakes he became poor, so that you through his poverty might become rich' (2 Cor. 8:9).

The Christians at Rome were not finding it easy to accept the principle of restricting the exercise of their Christian liberty where its exercise might cause another Christian, with a weaker conscience, to stumble. Once more, Paul appeals to the example of Christ: 'We who are strong ought to bear with the failings of the weak and not to please ourselves. Each of us should please his neighbour for his good to build him up. For even Christ did not please himself but, as it is written, "The insults of those who insult you have fallen on me"' (Rom. 15:1-3).

Christlikeness of conduct costs something. It frequently means the humbling of our pride, the disruption of our programme and the disturbing of our relaxation. But it remains irreplaceable, for it ultimately draws attention not so much to us but to what the Lord Jesus Christ is like, and what He is doing in our life. So often when Christlikeness is genuinely reflected someone will ask, 'Why do you react in that way?' Or, 'Why don't you lose your temper in that situation?' and humbly the answer may be given, 'As a Christian I try to be committed to the example of Jesus Christ' – and our Lord Jesus is praised and honoured in this way.

Every day is made up of choices and decisions – even for those of us whose lives appear the most humdrum. We have to decide how we are going to react to other people's needs, and often, perhaps, to their insensitivity to our own needs. We have to decide whether we are going to work hard or whether we are going to slack. We have to decide whether we are going to put our best into what we do, or simply get away with the minimum of effort. In all of these decisions – moment by moment – we either praise God by Christlikeness or we dishonour Him by neglecting to emulate His Son. While Christlikeness is impossible for us to achieve on our own, the gift of the Holy Spirit enables us to walk in our Lord's footsteps.

GIVING

We praise God in everyday life as we delight to be *generous*. 'Ascribe to the Lord the glory due to his name; bring an offering and come into his courts,' exhorts the psalmist (Ps. 96:8). It would be quite wrong to suggest that men and women of the world are ungenerous. But generosity is not a common feature of human nature. Money has to be coaxed out of people often by raffle tickets, sales of work, sweepstakes or charity concerts.

But Christian giving finds its starting point in how much it can give rather than in how little. It focuses upon God's generous giving, and it strives to express gratitude to God. When Mary 'took about a pint of pure nard, an expensive perfume' and 'poured it on Jesus' feet and wiped his feet with her hair' (John 12:3) she was expressing the gratitude every Christian feels and longs to express in tangible forms. Whenever we give to God's work we give in some way for the benefit of people. Not only does our giving itself express praise to God, but it calls forth praise to God too as many express their thanks to Him. In our giving to God we are tangibly expressing how much God means to us – which is nothing less than praise and worship.

One of the by-products of my daily employment is that it puts me in a position to be able to give. Let's work backwards for a moment in just one situation. Nothing brings greater praise to God than a man's discovery of God's salvation in the Lord Jesus Christ, with the result that he turns from living for himself to living for God's praise. But there are millions in the world who have never heard the message of God's salvation. And so it is that missionaries are called by God and are sent forth by His people, His church. But how are they to be supported? By the giving of God's people in proportion to how God prospers them in their daily work. Hence the praise of God from the lips and life of a converted Bornean tribesman is vitally linked with my earning my daily living and obtaining money. I can praise God in my everyday life by working to earn in order to give away. Everyday life finds meaning and point in every part as I realise that it can all be lived with God's praise in view.

As a modern song, translated from the German original, puts it:

> God's will for you is good,
> In the pattern of life
> Whatsoever each day may bring:
> Sing Him your song.
>
> God's will for you is good,
> Ev'ry morning anew
> Think upon His great faithfulness
> Sing Him your song.
>
> God's will for you is good,
> Stop to ponder again

All the blessings and gifts He gives:
Sing Him your song.

God's will for you is good,
Even sorrow and pain
Can bring blessing through His grace:
Sing Him your song.

God's will for you is good,
For He sent His own Son
To bear all our guilt and sin:
Sing Him your song.

God's will for you is good,
Be it sorrow or joy
He is faithful in life and death:
Sing Him your song.
(Gustav Bosse Verlag, Germany)

A PRAYER

Holy Father, thank You for helping me to understand that I can praise You as much in the ordinary affairs of life as in the unusual and more exciting things.

Thank You that through the Lord Jesus – and through Him alone – I can continually offer to You a sacrifice of praise. I want to praise You as much by my attitudes as by my words and my actions.

In the light of Your mercy to me, I want to do everything as for the Lord Jesus.

When pressures are on me not to trust You, help me to realise that then is the precise time that

I need to put my trust in You afresh and to praise Your saving power.

I commit myself now – with Your Spirit's help – to greater thankfulness, more wholehearted work, greater diligence in pursuing holiness and Christlikeness, and joy in giving; please bring greater praise to Your Name from my life by these and any other means You choose. For Jesus' sake.

Amen.

7

Praise in Death

I have before me the order of service for the funeral service of a good friend. It is not entitled a 'funeral' service, however, but a 'thanksgiving' service. On the last page there is a note to the effect that the order of service was prepared in detail by my friend two weeks before his death. And the hymns are hymns of praise, such as 'How good is the God we adore ...' and 'And can it be that I should gain an int'rest in the Saviour's blood?'

ARRANGEMENTS FOR PRAISE

It brings vividly to mind a pastoral call I made on an older couple whom we had first met in the course of a door-to-door visitation. The wife came first to faith in the Lord Jesus and the husband a little while later. The wife suffered dreadfully with cancer in its most advanced and devastating stages. But the Lord Jesus had become wonderfully precious in a very short Christian experience. When I made this call late on a Sunday evening I found the couple poring over the church hymn book. 'What are you doing?' I enquired. 'Choosing hymns for my *thanksgiving* service,' the wife replied. '*Thanksgiving* service?' I asked.

'Which service is that?' 'My funeral service, of course,' she answered. I stood rebuked that I had not cottoned on quickly to what she meant. The two hymns she chose were: 'To God be the glory! Great things he hath done' and 'All creatures of our God and King, lift up your voice and with us sing: Hallelujah, Hallelujah!' Such careful, God-glorifying preparation – where such is possible – is part of our praise of God in death.

AN ATTITUDE TO COVET

Charles Wesley captures the Christian's coveted attitude in the face of death:

> Happy, if with my latest breath
> I might but gasp His name;
> Preach Him to all, and cry in death:
> Behold, behold the Lamb!

Praise in death is perhaps the most difficult aspect of praise because none of us has yet experienced it. We must try to be neither sentimental nor unrealistic as we face its fierce reality.

Death is a horrible thing. The circumstances surrounding it may be most unpleasant in many cases. But one may believe that just as it is right to ask God for grace to live well it is also appropriate to ask God for grace to die well.

'This is the day of my coronation,' Perpetua, one of the early Christian martyrs from Carthaginia, said in A.D. 203 as her death approached. 'This is the day which the Lord hath made,' exclaimed James Guthrie the Covenanter, when he awoke in the morning of his execution in 1661, 'we will rejoice and be glad in it.' At different periods of the Christian Church's history believers have been able to affirm, 'Our men and women die well.'

JOHN BUNYAN'S INSIGHT

It must be admitted, however, that Christians do not always express the confidence that either Perpetua or James Guthrie exhibited. John Bunyan indicates that in *The Pilgrim's Progress* especially in his handling of the death of his two most prominent characters – Christian and his wife, Christiana. Christian's experience of the river of death was by no means a pleasant one initially. Christian and his friend, Hopeful, entered the waters together, and 'Christian began to sink; and, crying out to his good friend, Hopeful, he said, "I sink in deep waters; the billows go over my head; all the waves go over me."'

When Hopeful replied, 'Be of good cheer, my brother; I feel the bottom, and it is good.' Christian said, 'Ah! my friend, "the sorrows of death have compassed me about;" I shall not see the land that floweth with milk and honey.' And with that a great darkness and horror fell upon Christian, so that he could not see before him. Christian was troubled by the thoughts of the sins he had committed both since and before he became a Christian. As Hopeful quoted Scriptures to him, Christian was helped, but his passage through the river of death was nowhere so easy as Hopeful's.

In complete contrast was Christiana's death. When she realised that her time was near she called for Mr. Greatheart, her guide, and she asked him for his advice as to how best to prepare for her journey. Then 'she came forth and entered the river, with a beckon of farewell to those that followed her. The last words that she was heard to say were, 'I come, Lord, to be with thee, and bless thee!'" John Bunyan's accounts of the deaths of

Christian and Christiana remind us that Christians may have varying experiences at death and sometimes very different from what we might expect.

THE HOLY SPIRIT'S MINISTRY

The Holy Spirit is the Comforter, and He wants to fulfil His ministry to us in this capacity. His particular ministry as Comforter is to come alongside us in our trials so as to assure us that we are, in fact, more than conquerors over and in them all by our share in the victory of the Lord Jesus, and by the power of the Lord Jesus working in us by the Spirit.

He is the ideal Comforter because He actually dwells in us as believers. What the Lord Jesus did for His disciples by His presence with them, the Lord Jesus does for us by His Spirit who never leaves us, although we may grieve Him by our unbelief and disobedience.

Unfortunately, we can have false ideas of comfort. In human relationships someone who comforts is often someone who, finding us weeping or miserable, puts his or her arm round our shoulder, and says, 'There, now, don't upset yourself! Things may not be as bad as they look!' That friendly concern may be a comfort of sorts but it does not improve our situation. The Holy Spirit, however, in coming alongside us, effectively lifts our gaze to the Person of Christ, and assures us that nothing whatsoever can separate us from the love of Jesus Christ and the love of God our Father, and that we can even see our weakness, difficulty, or danger turned to the praise and glory of God. The Holy Spirit's comfort achieves something: it changes our outlook and our actions so that they bring praise to God.

A TRIUMPHANT DEATH AND ITS EXPLANATION

We must all have admired the example of the first Christian martyr, Stephen, whose story is told in Acts 6 and 7. The Bible goes to great pains to remind us that the outstanding men and women of God whose lives it relates were men and women just like ourselves (cf. James 5:17). Stephen feared stoning as much as any man. Just to pause a moment and consider what it must feel like to have sharp stones raining upon the whole of one's body makes one's flesh cringe. And yet Stephen's death proved a most triumphant occasion, for he was able to follow in his Master's footsteps and pray for his persecutors, 'Lord, do not hold this sin against them' (Acts 7:60).

The explanation of Stephen's behaviour in death lies with the Holy Spirit's ministry as the Comforter. Luke significantly begins his account of Stephen's final moments on earth with the words, 'But Stephen, *full of the Holy Spirit*, looked up to heaven and saw the glory of God, and Jesus standing at the right hand of God. "Look," he said, "I see heaven open and the Son of Man standing at the right hand of God"' (Acts 7:55, 56). The vision Stephen had into heaven itself was not by means of his natural eyes, but with the spiritual vision the Holy Spirit imparted as he filled Stephen's life with His grace and power.

Probably every Christian – on thinking about it seriously – would long to have the same vision at the moment of death; a vision of heaven and the glory of God, and Jesus standing at the right hand of God. It may not be the norm for Christians to have that kind of vision; we are not in a position to say. We know that

Stephen lived his life in dependence upon God's Spirit (cf. Acts 6:3), and it is no surprise that this was the Spirit's ministry to him at his death.

ENCOURAGING EXAMPLES

Many biographies reveal moments of special reassurance at the approach of death. Let me share two examples.

Sir Malcolm Sargent, the famous and popular conductor, was found to have cancer of the pancreas, and his case was hopeless. Although friends were given to understand that he had six months to live, he actually had only a fortnight. As Charles Reid tells the story in his biography:

> He used this respite to make his peace with God and take leave methodically of old friends. These he called to his bedside in considered sequence ... After the two days of shock and emotional readjustment, death came in prospect to wear the lineaments of a friend. He had long known intuitively and had sometimes proclaimed that this was how it would be. On his seventieth birthday he startled listeners to the BBC's Home Service by ebulliently declaring ... that death was something he looked forward to greatly. He had loved this life so much, he explained, that he knew he would love death still more. Then came a noble simile: 'When I go into the next world I shall not feel a stranger. As a child taken from the left breast cries only to find consolation in the right breast, so shall it be when we pass from life to death, from *life to life*.' During the last fortnight he had talks with Dr. Donald Coggan, the then Archbishop of York, who came to him both as a friend and a spiritual counsellor. Dr. Coggan has made known these deathbed words of his: 'I always had faith.

Now I have knowledge.' (Five days before his death he wrote to a younger friend.) 'I can assure you that it is a great privilege and advantage to have good notice.' (He phoned a colleague on the night of his death.) The Maestro's voice was clear and tranquil; he sounded happy. He said, 'I am slipping away peacefully. God bless you. Goodnight and goodbye' (Charles Reid: *Malcolm Sargent* p. 3ff).

BY SUCH A DEATH GOD IS PRAISED.

The second example is of a young married woman, who, with everything to live for humanly speaking, did not want to die. She was helped by a poem a friend wrote.

If everything is lost, thanks be to God
If I must see it go, watch it go,
Watch it fade away, die.
Thanks be to God that He is all I have
And if I have Him not, I have nothing at all
Nothing at all, only a farewell to the wind
Farewell to the grey sky
Goodbye, God be with you evening October sky.
If all is lost, thanks be to God,
For He is He, and I, I am only I.

She and her husband had prayed that she might not die in a coma. On the night of her death they prayed together in the hospital. And Davy – the wife – 'prayed aloud for the hospital and the doctors by name and the nurses ... in Jesus' name ... Then she said in a strange voice: "Oh, God, take me."' Her husband knew then that she was aware that she was dying. He writes,

I said: 'Go under the Love, dearling. Go under the Mercy.' She murmured: 'Amen.' And then she said:

'Thank you, blessed dearling ...' Suddenly her fingers tightened on mine. She said in a clear weak voice: 'Oh, dearling, look ...' She didn't go on, if there was more. I knew that if I said, 'What is it?' she would make an effort and go on; but I did not do so. I don't know why I didn't. She might have been saying 'look' as one who suddenly understands something, or as one who beholds – what? Her voice was so frail, I could not tell which it was. I wished very much to know: I could have asked her; I did not. And I shall not know this side of eternity, for they were her last words: 'Oh, dearling, look' (Sheldon Vanauken: *A Severe Mercy*, p. 163, 174f).

A general promise, relating to the whole of the Christian's life, may well prove true at the Christian's death. The Lord Jesus promises, 'Whoever has my commands and obeys them, he is the one who loves me. He who loves me will be loved by my Father, and I too will love him and show myself to him' (John 14:21). If our Lord does choose to show Himself to us at the time of our departure, it will certainly cause us to praise Him. If he does not, we shall have cause to praise Him when our departure is complete and we are in His presence, and we shall understand His dealings with us (1 Cor. 13:12). As our constant companion, the Holy Spirit knows when we most need the encouragement of Christ's revelation to our soul – and we may trust Him to do what is best for us, as we strive to live in obedience to the Lord Jesus.

'FATHER'S TRAIN TICKET'

Corrie ten Boom tells how, as a young girl, she visited a home where a baby had died. For the first time death became a reality. Curiosity and terror struggled in her.

That night she crept into bed beside her sister Nollie. That night as their father stepped through the door, Corrie burst into tears. 'I need you!' she sobbed. 'You can't die! You can't!' Her sister explained their visit to the dead child's home.

Their father sat down on the edge of the narrow bed. 'Corrie,' he began gently, 'when you and I go to Amsterdam – when do I give you your ticket?' She sniffed a few times, considering this. 'Why, just before we get on the train.' 'Exactly. And our wise Father in heaven knows when we're going to need things, too. Don't run ahead of Him, Corrie. When the time comes that some of us will have to die, you will look into your heart and find the strength you need – just in time' (Corrie ten Boom: *The Hiding Place*, p. 31f).

The lesson was not lost, for the time came when Corrie's aunt was confirmed as having a terminal illness. Corrie's father took the family with him hoping they might console her by reminding her of the full life she had lived and the many good works she had done. But their well-meant words were empty. She put her hands over her eyes and began to cry. 'Empty, empty!' She choked at last through the tears, 'How can we bring anything to God? What does he care for our little tricks and trinkets?' And then as they listened in disbelief, 'she lowered her hands and with tears coursing down her face whispered, "Dear Jesus, I thank you that you have done all – all – on the Cross, and that all we need in life or death is to be sure of this."' Corrie ten Boom says that she stood rooted to the spot, knowing that she had seen a mystery. 'It was Father's train ticket, given at the moment itself' (Corrie ten Boom: *The Hiding Place*, p. 41f).

FLUCTUATING EMOTIONS

It is impossible for any one of us to say what our own feelings will really be at the moment of death, because even now our views of it change.

John Newton put his finger on our fluctuating feelings when he wrote:

> Our view of death will not always be alike, but in proportion to the degree in which the Holy Spirit is pleased to communicate His sensible influence. We may anticipate the moment of dissolution with pleasure and desire in the morning, and be ready to shrink from the thought of it before night. But though our frames and perceptions vary, the report of faith concerning it is the same. The Lord usually reserves dying strength for a dying hour ... but when the time shall arrive which He has appointed for your dismission, I make no doubt but He will overpower all your fears, silence all your enemies, and give you a comfortable, triumphant entrance into His kingdom. You have nothing to fear from death: for Jesus, by dying, has disarmed it of its sting, has perfumed the grave, and opened the gates of glory for His believing people. Satan, so far as he is permitted, will assault our peace, but he is a vanquished enemy: our Lord holds him in a chain, and sets him bounds which he cannot pass. He provides for us likewise the whole armour of God and has promised to cover our heads Himself in the day of battle, to bring us honourably through every skirmish, and to make us more than conquerors at last.

PREPARING OURSELVES

There is a sense in which we need to prepare ourselves to die well. Now this is the opposite of morbidity! I'm not suggesting that we go round with a dismal look on our face, proclaiming, 'I may die any minute and I must be ready!' But rather like a soldier who trains in advance for hazards that are going to be before him, in order that his reactions will be right at the time, we should remind ourselves in the present of the truths upon which we should stay our lives when the moment of death arrives.

Of course, the manner in which death may come is capable of innumerable permutations.

Death may come for some of us after a period of senility when we may be completely oblivious of our circumstances and the approach of our death. Death may come for others of us in our sleep or by sudden accident.

On the other hand, it may be surrounded by intense pain and suffering when the urgent needs of the body for relief overwhelm the soul's awareness of God and there may seem to be little room for praise.

But if it is to be our lot consciously to face death without such distressing circumstances – or, for that matter, with them – we need to think of preparing ourselves to die well.

GOD'S CHARACTER

Rather like a three-legged stool, there are three main areas of revelation which encourage the Christian to face death with praise. The first is God's revelation of Himself. Let us take just three aspects of His character: His eternity, His love and His sovereignty.

First, let's consider an illustration of His eternity, and its significance. When God made Himself known to Moses He said, 'I am the God of ... Abraham, the God of Isaac, and the God of Jacob' (Exod. 3:6; Matt. 22:32). In other words, he did not say, 'I *was* the God of Abraham, the God of Isaac and the God of Jacob.' Taking up this statement, our Lord went on to say, 'He is not the God of the dead but of the living' (Matt. 22:32). God not only lives forever but He imparts eternal life to His people. Abraham, Isaac and Jacob are not dead, but alive! We too cannot be united to God in Christ without sharing God's life – we have been given the privilege of participating in the divine nature (2 Pet. 1:3).

Secondly, God has revealed His love to us in His dear Son, our Lord Jesus Christ. We may exclaim like Paul, 'What, then, shall we say in response to this? If God is for us, who can be against us? He who did not spare his own Son, but gave him up for us all – how will he not also, along with him, graciously give us all things?' (Rom. 8:31, 32).

One of the wonders of God's love is that it holds us in its sure embrace for ever. Paul provides a catalogue of things which would seemingly threaten us: trouble, hardship, persecution, famine, nakedness, danger, sword, angels, demons, things in the present and things in the future, including death, with the triumphant conclusion that nothing is able to separate us from the love of God that is in Christ Jesus our Lord (Rom. 8:35-39). Think of the thickest and strongest rope imaginable, and then remember that God binds you to Himself by the rope of His love, a rope which cannot be severed. When death approaches, it is time to ponder anew that love, for the love that has surrounded us in life becomes all the more precious in death.

Thirdly, God has revealed His sovereignty to us. 'My times are in your hands,' declared the psalmist

(Ps. 31:15). Many of our anxieties about death concern not ourselves but those whom we love. While death can only bring joy to the believer, it invariably brings a great measure of sorrow to those who are left behind. But God's sovereignty and love are in perfect harmony. He knows the end from the beginning; He knows what is best for both those whom we love and for ourselves. 'Who of you by worrying,' our Lord asked, 'can add a single hour to his life?' (Matt. 6:27). Confidence in God's sovereignty means that we do not have to worry about our life-span, but that rather our preoccupation should be to live well, and then we shall die well.

William Freeman Lloyd's hymn is presented often as a rather mournful hymn of submission to God but, in fact, it is a joyful hymn of confidence, expressing Christians' wisdom as they pray –

> My times are in Thy hand:
> My God, I wish them there;
> My life, my friends, my soul I leave
> Entirely to Thy care.
>
> My times are in Thy hand:
> Why should I doubt or fear?
> My Father's hand will never cause
> His child a needless tear.
>
> My times are in Thy hand:
> I'll always trust in Thee;
> And, after death, at Thy right hand
> I shall for ever be.

God's eternity, love and sovereignty are only three of many attributes of God upon which we should meditate, but they illustrate how much we have to praise God for concerning Himself, both in life and death.

CHRIST'S VICTORY

The second ground for our praise of God in death is His Son's victory over death. Just as He stood before Martha at the death of her brother, He stands before us, and says, 'I am the resurrection and the life. He who believes in me will live, even though he dies; and whoever lives and believes in me will never die' (John 11:25, 26).

By the grace of God the Lord Jesus tasted death for us. Standing in our place as our Substitute, He endured the rod of God's righteous judgment upon Him to the end that we might not have to endure it. He drank the cup of God's righteous wrath against sin that we might not have to drink it. None has suffered as He suffered when He became the atoning sacrifice for our sins, and 'not only for ours but also for the sins of the whole world' (1 John 2:2). Wonderfully and gloriously, God the Father raised Him from the dead on the third day, thereby declaring the identity of His Son and the completion of His saving work.

But even more good flows from His work on our behalf. God declares that sharing in Christ's death we also share in His Son's Resurrection. Faith brings us into the closest possible union with Christ – we are actually described as being 'in Christ'. Even as He was raised from the dead by the power of God's Spirit, so too at Christ's coming shall our bodies be raised to life, transformed and made like Christ's own glorious body (Phil. 3:21). And so it is that we share not only in His death and Resurrection, but in His Ascension also. Already, in principle, we may say that

'God raised us up with Christ and seated us with him in the heavenly realms in Christ Jesus, in order that in the coming ages he might show the incomparable riches of his grace, expressed in his kindness to us in Christ Jesus' (Eph. 2:6, 7).

Because the Lord Jesus is the Resurrection and the Life, those who believe in Him can never really die. While we must pass through physical death, it is without the sting of death being present any more, and with the assurance that death will usher our spirits into the presence of God, and that after death there is the certain prospect of resurrection life. Just as He said to John, our Lord says to us, 'Do not be afraid. I am the First and the Last. I am the Living One; I was dead, and behold I am alive for ever and ever! And I hold the keys of death and Hades' (Rev. 1:17, 18). Keys symbolise authority, and those who belong to Christ need never fear death, for their Master has complete authority over it. What a cause for praise!

DEATH TRANSFORMED

The third ground for our praise of God in death is the transformation our Lord's saving work has brought to it. Death means 'going home'. Living the Christian life as we ought, we learn to set our hearts on things above, where Christ is seated at the right hand of God (Col. 3:1), for that is where He has gone to prepare a place for us (John 14:2, 3). While this is picture language and we cannot guess with any certainty all it really means, we have the assurance that no eye has seen, no ear has heard, no mind has conceived what God has prepared for those who love him (Isa. 64:4; 1 Cor. 2:9), and the Holy

Spirit creates a great deal of anticipation within us at the prospect. We need no more fear death than we fear going home after a period of absence.

A young minister 'was called to the bedside of an elderly woman who was approaching the end of her life. He tried to comfort her, and muttered something about how sorry he was that she had to die, when she interrupted, "God bless you, young man, there's nothing to be scairt about. I'm just going to cross over Jordan in a few hours, and my Father owns the land on both sides of the river"' (D.J. Fant: *AW Tozer*, p. 169).

Every Christian's death is a moment of triumph. Peter refers to his own impending death as his 'departure' and the Greek word he employs is 'exodus' (2 Pet. 1:15). It was about our Lord's exodus that Moses and Elijah spoke to Him on the occasion of the Transfiguration (Luke 9:31). Now our Lord's death, though cruel and devastating, was triumphant, for by it He achieved the salvation of His people (Matt. 1:21). Our union with Christ is so complete that we enter completely into His triumph. In the Old Testament the Exodus was an occasion of supreme triumph, for God's people passed out of bondage into liberty. Death marks the believer's exodus – he or she leaves the bondage which marks so much of human existence in the world to enjoy the freedom of God's immediate presence.

At certain stages in life it is fun to enjoy a camping holiday. But what a relief it is, no matter how enjoyable the holiday, to be back in one's proper home. At death Christians simply exchange their earthly tent for an eternal house in the heavens (2 Cor. 5:1ff), and they can have no complaints about that.

But the vital transformation of death for believers is that instead of frightening them, it holds the prospect of being with Christ whom they love. The more we enjoy Christ in this life, the more we anticipate with joy the life to come. 'For to me, to live is Christ,' declared Paul, 'and to die is gain. If I am to go on living in the body, this will mean fruitful labour for me. Yet what shall I choose? I do not know! I am torn between the two: I desire to depart and be with Christ, which is better by far' (Phil. 1:21-23). Paul underlines here the truth of the believer's immediate experience of the presence of Christ at the moment of death. To be absent from the body is to be present with the Lord – and consciously present with Him. If death means awaiting the Second Coming of the Lord Jesus and the great Resurrection of the dead before the realisation of some of heaven's glories there would have been no point in Paul writing that 'to die is gain'. But he had the assurance that what he had seen Stephen bear witness to would be his own experience, as that of every believer: the Lord Jesus standing ready to welcome him into His presence.

The soul is able to praise God as it rests on the certainties God has revealed – the certainties of His own character, His Son's saving work, and the transformation of death promised in the gospel. When the scientist Michael Faraday, lay dying, he was asked, 'What are your speculations?' He replied, 'Speculations? I have none. I rest my soul on certainties.'

LEANING ON HIS STAFF

Jacob provides us with an Old Testament example of dying well, an example the New Testament recognises: 'By faith Jacob, when he was dying, blessed each of

Joseph's sons, and worshipped as he leaned on the top of his staff' (Heb. 11:21; cf. Gen. 48, 49).

As Jacob became aware of the fact that he was dying, he worshipped. He was able to praise God, first, for His past dealings with him – and his staff was a symbol of those dealings. When Jacob had prayed before meeting up once more with Esau, he had made reference to his staff: 'I am unworthy of all the kindness and faithfulness you have shown your servant. I had only my staff when I crossed this Jordan, but now I have become two camps' (Gen. 32:10). That staff came to symbolise even more to him after his wrestling with God at the place called Peniel, because ever after 'he was limping because of his hip' (Gen. 32:31) and he needed the regular support of his staff.

Secondly, Jacob was able to praise God for the fact that he was a pilgrim going home. Giving testimony to Pharaoh not long before his death, he declared, 'The years of my pilgrimage are a hundred and thirty. My years have been few and difficult, and they do not equal the years of the pilgrimage of my fathers' (Gen. 47:9).

A young Christian once met C. S. Lewis for lunch and they talked about death, or rather awakening after death. They agreed that it would be 'a sort of coming home'. The young Christian and his wife were leaving for the U.S.A., their home, and C.S. Lewis expressed the wish that they might come back to England. '"At all events," he said with a cheerful grin, "we'll certainly meet again here – or there."' They shook hands and C.S. Lewis said, 'I shan't say goodbye. We'll meet again.' Having crossed to the other side of the road, 'he raised his voice in a great roar that easily overcame the noise of the cars and buses. Heads turned and at least one car swerved. "Besides," he bellowed with a great grin, "Christians never say goodbye!'" (Sheldon Vanauken: *A Severe Mercy*, p. 125). A pilgrim knows that his destination is beyond this life; and Jacob was able to praise God for this assurance as he leaned on his staff.

Finally, Jacob was able to praise God that His purposes would be fulfilled by those following on after him. Chapters 48 and 49 of Genesis record the blessings he pronounced in God's name upon each of Joseph's sons and it was only after 'Jacob had finished giving instructions to his sons, he drew his feet up into the bed, breathed his last and was gathered to his people' (Gen. 49:33). It is a cause for praise in death that the work in which God has given us a part will not cease because of our departure, but others – one with us in Christ – will take it up, generation after generation, until the work is done and the Lord returns.

'The path of the righteous is like the first gleam of dawn, shining ever brighter till the full light of day,' declares the writer of Proverbs (4:18). If we may apply that for a moment to the believer's death, 'the full light of day' will be when we come into the presence of the Lord, and then 'there will be no more death or mourning or crying or pain, for the old order of things has passed away' (Rev. 21:4).

Then –

> I'll bless the hand that guided,
> I'll bless the heart that planned,
> When throned where glory dwelleth
> In Immanuel's land.

But we do not have to wait until then, for 'I will extol the LORD at all times; his praise will always be on my lips'

(Ps. 34:1) – including by the Spirit's help, the moment of my exodus!

A POSTSCRIPT

Our preoccupation has been with the Christian's praise in death, and much of what we have said will be relevant to the Christian in bereavement. But praise in bereavement is far from easy. We should not pretend that it is.

If, however, the one who died was a believer, there is room for praise. The sorrow we feel is not then sorrow without hope. The loss we feel is not for ever – and the measure of our loss is the measure of what God gave us in the relationship we now miss. While death has come in the midst of love, love has not died. God is to be praised, therefore, for all that He gave us in the person we loved so much and the lovely prospect of reunion may rightly thrill our hearts.

Christ's presence may be made all the more real to us in our loneliness. He does not leave us desolate. He will guide us all our remaining days and bring us to glory. Is He not to be praised for this? And the one we love is beyond the reach of sorrow. Our loss has been all gain for him or her. Loneliness, desolation and perplexity are past for that person. The victory of our Lord Jesus Christ is celebrated every time a Christian anywhere dies – therefore, we may praise. That does not mean that praise is easy, but its very difficulty makes the praise all the more great and meaningful.

John Newton – the author of the hymn 'Amazing Grace' – confessed that when his wife died 'the world seemed to die with her'. Nevertheless he preached on the Sunday following her death on Habakkuk 3:17-18 and wrote a hymn suitable for the occasion. Two of the verses went as follows,

> Domestic joys, alas, how rare!
> Possess'd, and known by few!
> And they who know them, find they are
> As frail and transient too.
>
> But you, who love the Saviour's voice,
> And rest upon His name,
> Amidst these changes may rejoice,
> For He is still the same.

Whatever else we say to ourselves in bereavement, this is our anchor – 'He is still the same' – and this assurance is an unceasing cause for praise.

A Prayer

Lord, if I'm honest I wonder sometimes how I will face up to the moment of death. I would hate to let You down or to be unhelpful to those who witness my departure.

But I thank You that perfect love casts out fear and that Your love which has redeemed and kept me will sustain me to the end. May Your grace strengthen me also in my dying hour to praise You, whether it be soon or many years from now. May the last word be with You and not with my great enemy, Satan.

Help me so to cultivate and value fellowship with the Lord Jesus in the present that I may even view death as a friend in disguise because it will usher me into my Saviour's nearer presence. Amen.

8

Praise in Heaven

Praise in heaven is obviously the place to end, but it could just as easily have been the place to begin. God made us for Himself, and in heaven we shall fulfil the glorious purpose of our creation – we shall enjoy God forever. And those who enjoy God praise Him continually. As the psalmist so aptly puts it, 'In his temple all cry, "Glory!"' (Ps. 29:9). 'Heaven,' wrote Martin Luther, 'is heaven not because joy is there, but because the praise of God is there, as Psalm 84:4 states: "Blessed are those who dwell in your house; they are for ever praising you." For God gives them pleasure, and for this reason they rejoice.'

FULL DEVELOPMENT
Some acts of worship – such as the Lord's Supper – undoubtedly belong to this life alone, and they will cease as soon as we enter into heaven. But praise will be our eternal employment. Our praise of God will reach its full development in heaven. John tells how he heard 'what sounded like the roar of a great multitude in heaven shouting: "Hallelujah! Salvation and glory and power belong to our God, for true and just are his judgments ..."'

He heard a voice 'from the throne, saying: "Praise our God, all you his servants, you who fear him, both great and small!"' Once more he heard 'what sounded like a great multitude, like the roar of rushing waters and like loud peals of thunder, shouting: "Hallelujah! For our Lord God Almighty reigns. Let us rejoice and be glad and give him glory!"' (Rev. 19:1, 2, 5, 6, 7).

My ears can recapture the sound of the mighty roar of an enthusiastic audience as they express their applause, or of a vast congregation singing at the top of their voices, led by a powerful choir. The enthusiastic roar of heaven's inhabitants' praise, however, surpasses all the world has ever known! Furthermore, it is unceasing, for, as we are told, the living creatures around God's throne never stop saying, 'Holy, holy, holy is the Lord God Almighty, who was, and is, and is to come.' (Rev. 4:8).

RESERVE

The Bible shows reserve, however, in its descriptions of heaven, and understandably so. How can you explain to a goldfish in its bowl what it is like to be as free as a bird in the sky? How do you describe a tropical fruit to someone who has never tasted it? Or a sunset to a man born blind? Or a Beethoven symphony to someone born deaf? I read somewhere of an American city street urchin who was taken for the first time to the country and who saw a songbird perched on a branch. 'Poor little bird,' said the five-year-old city waif, 'poor little bird, he has no cage to live in.' The only songbirds he knew were kept in cages! His understanding was governed by the life he knew, and that limited understanding caused him to make mistakes in his assessment of life outside his environment.

DIFFICULTY

We do not find it easy to visualise life in heaven. Sometimes our mental images are distorted by unhelpful childhood conceptions based on drawings and paintings and exaggerated symbolism. Although hearing a sermon on heaven or reading a book about it may create excitement in our heart, we may find that when we try to imagine ourselves there we find mental images extremely difficult. We are not alone in this – it's normal. But we need to remember that our confidence in heaven lies not in our power to visualise it but in the total reliability of the One who promises it to us.

We may wonder, therefore, if there is any value in considering the praise of heaven. There are at least two grounds for doing so. First, the Book of Revelation provides us with glimpses of heaven's worship, and since that praise is perfect praise, it guides us in our present praise of God. We should aim at making our present praise of God the closest possible approximation to what we know heaven's praise to be. Secondly, the contemplation of heaven – like a traveller looking at pictures of his home country – should make us homesick for heaven, our true home. One of the earliest uses of the word 'nostalgia' is in Captain Cook's journals of his voyages, where it is used as a medical term to describe the sailors' longing for home as they looked forward to their homeward journey. Obviously the more we set before our souls the glorious position they shall enjoy before long, the more 'nostalgic' they will probably be, and the more they will be in love with the prospect.

Our souls never function better than when they are stirred up by some praiseworthy desire and affection.

SOMETHING GREATER

The simple word 'plus' has come to my mind as I have thought of the praise of heaven. However I anticipate it, it will be greater. However I try to describe it, it will be so much better. It will be plus all we can think, ask or imagine, as is always the case with our great God and Saviour (Eph. 3:20).

Our praise will be greater because of our increased understanding. We know already that we do not deserve the place our Saviour reserves for us in heaven, so God's grace causes us to praise Him. But our praise will be all the greater in heaven itself because then we shall really understand how unworthy of ourselves we are to be there (cf. Matt. 25:37) and our total dependence upon God's grace in Christ.

As sheep of the Great Shepherd, we shall appreciate the full extent of the Shepherd's sacrifice in laying aside heaven's glories and becoming man, and suffering for our sins.

We shall comprehend more fully our dependence on God. We shall live as we ought to have lived on earth, in full and perfect dependence upon God, the source of all being, life, goodness and happiness.

GOD'S PRESENCE

Our praise will be greater because we shall always be in God's immediate presence. The redeemed 'are before the throne of God and serve him day and night in his temple; and he who sits on the throne will spread his tent over them' (Rev. 7:15). John tells how he heard a loud voice saying, 'Now the dwelling of God is with men, and he will live with them. They will be his people, and God himself will be with them and be their God' (Rev. 21:3).

Many experiences of God's grace cause us to praise Him now, but none causes us to praise Him more than the awareness He gives us from time to time of His presence. As Samuel Rutherford put it, when imprisoned for the sake of the gospel, 'Jesus Christ came into my cell last night, and every stone flashed like a ruby.' However, in heaven God's presence will be our continual experience. We shall not only have His nearness at certain special occasions, but we shall be continually in His presence in raptures of joy and praise.

SIGHT

Our praise will be greater because of sight. 'Here' we walk by faith, but 'there' we shall walk by sight. As John Bunyan's Mr. Stand-fast stood halfway in Jordan's river, he said, 'I have formerly lived by hearsay and faith, but now I go where I shall live by sight, and shall be with Him, in whose company I delight.' One of the marked differences of heaven's praise compared with our present praise will be our vision of God. In our present state we cannot look with our natural eyes upon God (Exod. 33:20; John 1:18), but in our future state it will be our privilege and the source of our eternal happiness and praise.

This is sometimes called 'the beatific vision', by which is meant that the enjoyment of heaven will be the sight of God's glory, especially as it is revealed in our Lord Jesus Christ. The most helpful writer on the subject of heaven I know is John Owen, the seventeenth-century Puritan. Unfortunately his manner of writing is so different from contemporary writing that it takes much time and effort to get 'tuned' into it, but he makes a most helpful point when he writes:

God in His immense essence is invisible unto our corporeal (i.e. physical) eyes, and will be so to eternity: as also incomprehensible unto our minds. For nothing can comprehend that which is infinite but what is itself infinite. Wherefore the blessed and blessed sight we shall have of God will be always 'in the face of Jesus Christ'. Therein will that manifestation of the glory of God, in His infinite perfections and all their blessed operations, so shine into our souls, as shall immediately fill us with peace, rest and glory' (Owen, I, p. 292, 293).

Perhaps we may not have thought before of the possibility that we shall see the glory of God for ever in the face of Jesus Christ. But it makes sense the more one thinks of it. How better could the Father honour the Son? And how it will cause us to praise the Father and the Son! And surely this is one of Spirit's purposes in bringing us finally to glory.

Here and now our sight of Christ's glory is by occasional glances and glimpses, whether in worship, prayer, the reading of the Scriptures or through the preaching of God's Word. Our spiritual vision is all too imperfect and partial. But in heaven it will immediate, direct and perfect. The Lord Jesus will never withdraw Himself from our sight.

LOVE

Our praise will be greater in heaven because of perfect love. In this world we are united to God by faith. It is by means of faith that we are taught to hold fast to Him. And, of course, we love Him too, and it is our love which further prompts us to praise Him. Yet our love is often fluctuating and feeble, making our praise spasmodic and weak.

But in heaven we shall be united to God by love. We shall have such a clear apprehension and grasp of God's infinite goodness and beauty that we shall always delight in Him and rejoice in Him, holding fast to Him with an ardent love – a perfect and unfluctuating affection.

Realising as never before the perfection of God's love, in all its gigantic dimensions, we shall love Him to our fullest capacity – and praise Him accordingly.

GLORY

Our praise will be greater in heaven because of our sight of Christ's glory. Our Lord prayed, 'Father, I want those you have given me to be with me where I am, and to see my glory, the glory you have given me because you loved me before the creation of the world' (John 17:24).

We shall see perfectly what the disciples caught only a glimpse of at our Lord's Transfiguration. We shall possess a perfect sight of the glory of His divine Person, which is absolutely the same as that of the Father. We'll praise Him! We shall see the glorified state of His human nature. We shall see His body in which He suffered for us and underwent all sorts of reproaches and troubles. And we shall praise Him! We shall see the particular glory the Father has given to Him as Mediator, and understand all that it means when the Bible says that the Father has given Him the Name above every name. And we'll praise Him!

To catch a glimpse of Christ's glory now makes us want to praise God with hearts that feel as if they could burst. What superior praise will come from our hearts and lips as we comprehend all at once the glory of Christ's love and condescension, the full extent of His union with His church, and the manner in which the glory of God's wisdom, righteousness, grace, love, goodness and power all shine forth eternally in Him!

GLORIFICATION

Our praise will be greater in heaven because of our glorification. One of the greatest hindrances to our praise of God now are the limitations imposed by our physical bodies and the waywardness of our sinful flesh. But in heaven our transformed bodies will be the perfect vehicle for our new nature. Here and now we 'live in houses of clay, whose foundations are in the dust, who are crushed more readily than a moth! Between dawn and dusk they are broken to pieces; unnoticed, they perish for ever' (Job 4:19, 20). We look up at the lights of the sky – the sun, the moon and the stars – and they emphasise our smallness and insignificance (Ps. 8:3). It hardly seems possible that we should entertain thoughts of being carried and exalted above them. But that is to be our experience. We are to share our Lord's glory – we shall be like Him (1 John 3:2).

Whatever the Bible means by our bodies being 'glorified' or transformed so as to be like Christ's glorious body (Phil. 3:21), it certainly means we shall be freed from all the flesh's hampering aspects and unhelpful influences. We shall be completely purified from all tendencies to instability and inclinations to sensuality and temptation. Our bodies will be completely suited to the spiritual activities of our souls in their highest exercise in response to the glory of God – praise!

Reunion and fellowship

Our praise in heaven will be greater because of reunion and fellowship. Relationships in Jesus Christ are so valuable and meaningful in this life that when we meet together, we so often praise God for His goodness to us in Christian fellowship, and in the precious relationships we enjoy in Christ. But what of heaven, and the praise of reunion and then of unbroken fellowship together? What a glorious rendezvous heaven will be, for it will be the most wonderful family gathering we can imagine!

The apostle Paul implied in his letters that he would have a knowledge of his readers when he entered into heaven. He wrote, for example, to the Thessalonians, 'For what is our hope, our joy, or the crown in which we will glory in the presence of our Lord Jesus Christ when he comes? Is it not you? Indeed, you are our glory and joy' (1 Thess. 2:19, 20). We have no idea of the means of this distinct knowledge of one another. We do not know if by means of our glorified senses we shall recognise one another's glorified bodies, or whether we shall know one another by immediate revelation after the manner in which Peter, James and John seemed to recognise Moses and Elijah at our Lord's Transfiguration. But know one another we shall!

What praise the joy of spending heaven with those we have loved and admired will prompt. The sadness we have known in parting will be more than recompensed because of eternal reunion. We shall have an everlasting enjoyment of one another.

Having spent an evening with friends who had taken the trouble to travel some distance to see him, George Whitefield wrote that night in his diary, 'Oh, how does their sweet company cause me to long for communion among the spirits of just men made perfect!'

REWARDS

Our praise will be greater in heaven because of rewards. Richard Sibbes put it well when he wrote, 'There will be a resurrection of credits, as well as of bodies.' When we live the Christian life as we ought, we want no reward save that of pleasing God. The greatest benefit God can give us is to know more of Himself.

When the Bible talks of rewards it exercises considerable restraint. But it assures us that there will be rewards in heaven for faithful service rendered in this present life, and some of our Lord's parables had instruction on this subject as part of their main thrust. But rewards are not to be thought of as wages. Rather they are the surprises that a loving Father gives to His children, and they will take all who receive them by surprise (Matt. 25:37ff). They will be rewards of grace. None of us will feel that he or she deserves them – for we shall then perfectly know the truth that we do not - but that realisation will make us praise God all the more. 'It has been worth it all!' will be the conviction and tribute of martyrs and all who have been persecuted for the sake of the gospel. Having done the will of God on earth, we will have received what He promised, and our confidence will have been richly rewarded (Heb. 10:35, 36).

PERFECTION

Our praise will be greater in heaven because of the perfection of all God provides for us. Two little words – *no more* ... ' – express something of the wonder of that perfection. Millions in the world today suffer hunger and thirst. Refugees and displaced persons wander here and there seeking refuge. Bitter experiences come to all, bringing tears and often the tears of mourning. Pain may dog our footsteps, and peril may be more acute during the night. But in heaven there will be no more hunger, no more thirst, no more wandering, no more tears, no more mourning, no more pain, and no more night (Rev. 7:16, 17; 21:4, 5).

When Dr. Alexander Whyte was minister of Free St. George's in Edinburgh a new organist, Mr. Alfred Hollins, took up the responsibility of leading the congregation's praise. He found that the slowness of the pneumatic action in the organ caused an appreciable interval between the pressing of the key and the giving forth of the sound . He mentioned on one occasion that this made it difficult to lead the singing effectively, or to play rapid passages, never imagining that Dr. Whyte particularly noted what he said. Some years later, when preaching on the perfect condition to which we may look forward in heaven for the prosecution of work or art, Dr. Whyte added as an illustration, 'And Mr. Hollins will have an organ which will answer to the slightest touch of his fingers!' Everything in heaven will be a cause for praise for it will demonstrate the perfection of its Architect.

SATISFACTION

Our praise in heaven will be greater most of all because of the unexcelled satisfaction we shall enjoy in God Himself. Imagine a thirsty man being brought to an ocean of pure drinking water – he has enough. And yet in heaven there will be no sense of our having too much satisfaction and no sense of weariness with it, but our satisfaction will be everlastingly new and fresh. Fresh joys spring from God continually. He is as much to be desired after millions of years – and, of necessity I have to use language that will be irrelevant in heaven where time, as we now know it, will have ceased – than when we first experienced the satisfaction of heaven. The praise we shall give will be continually fresh as a consequence.

'Now this is eternal life,' our Saviour said as He prayed to the Father, 'that they may know you, the only true God, and Jesus Christ, whom you have sent' (John 17:3). Our knowledge of God and our fellowship with Him, will be perfectly satisfying. 'And I,' the psalmist avowed, 'in righteousness I shall see your face; when I awake, I shall be satisfied with seeing your likeness' (Ps. 17:15). It is our Lord Jesus alone who is the likeness and image of God, and when we awake in the eternal world, with our minds purified and our souls equipped for eternity, knowing God and having fellowship with Him, will be always satisfying and exciting to us. We shall enjoy Him for ever – and praise him for ever!

DOWN TO EARTH!

However, we are not 'there', but 'here'. Our enjoyment of God for ever is to be preceded by our glorifying Him now. But our somewhat clumsy anticipation of heaven – and it cannot but be clumsy – does provoke us to more intelligent praise in the present.

The praise of heaven, as revealed to us in the Book of Revelation, for example, constitutes a guide for our present praise of God. Since the praise of heaven is unceasing, we should aim at making our praise of God as unceasing as possible, and not least by the manner in which we try to live to God's praise.

In praising God, we should concentrate upon giving Him glory, honour and thanks (Rev. 4:9). All glory is already God's, and in one sense we cannot give Him glory. But the giving of glory to God is the acknowledgement on our part of God's glory. We give glory to God as we draw attention to His attributes, to His character, and express our appreciation of Him. When we give glory to God we take time to ponder His revelation of Himself, and we respond in grateful, adoring praise.

Honour follows closely upon glory. When we rightly ponder God's being we find ourselves saying, in a variety of ways, 'Who would not fear and reverence You, Lord, for there is no one else like You in holiness, righteousness, judgment and glory?' While true praise, therefore, is joyful, it is also reverent – and in true praise there is no conflict between joy and reverence.

Thanks inevitably follow glory and honour. The wonder of God's salvation is that He the all-glorious, ever-to-be-revered Lord has visited us in His Son and has redeemed us to Himself, and actually made us His sons and daughters, heirs of heaven itself. The Holy One declares us holy; the Righteous One imputes to us the righteousness of His own Son; the Judge of all the earth declares us just in His sight; and the Glorious One makes us partakers of His glory. How can any believer's heart and lips be dumb?

THE CENTRE

At the centre of all our praise to God, therefore, should be the Person and work of His Son as the Lamb of God:

'Worthy is the Lamb, who was slain, to receive power and wealth and wisdom and strength and honour and glory and praise!' (Rev. 5:12). And in praising the Lamb we should remember that we also praise the Father for He gave and sent the Son into the world to be our Saviour.

The theme of victory also has a proper place in our praise. Probably because of the context of persecution within which the Book of Revelation was written, considerable attention focuses upon the Son's victory – a victory He shares with His people. The conflicts and trials of this present life are seen not to be final. The Church's anticipated and certain victory in the future has its foundations laid in the victory already won by our Lord Jesus. The world powers may sometimes win battles (Rev. 11:7; 13:7), but their victories are fleeting ones. In the end it is the Lamb who will be totally triumphant. In the middle of John's picture of the plagues and the wrath of God he sees the victors standing in heaven, singing a hymn of praise (Rev. 15:3ff). The victory which the Lamb has won, and which He has promised to His people, is already secure: for He is King of all kings and Lord of all lords (Rev. 17:14). Even now heaven's praise anticipates that victory, and when heaven's inhabitants are complete they will for ever praise the Lamb for His triumph over all their enemies.

THE BEST IS YET TO BE!

Finally, we should praise God for the anticipation of heaven we have even as we now think of it. The indwelling Holy Spirit is God's pledge to us that we shall finally arrive there with unspeakable joy, and –

Praise in Heaven

Then shall I see and hear and know
All I desired or wished below
And every power find sweet employ
In that eternal world of joy.
(Isaac Watts)

A PRAYER

Father of glory, how I thank You for the assurance of heaven! While I know I could never deserve such an assurance, I'm so grateful that You even give it to me as a right because of my union with Your Son, my Saviour. Thank You that while I live in the world I can seek to serve You fruitfully, and to praise You by the kind of life I live, as well as by my lips.

I long to give glory, honour and thanks to You always. May Your indwelling Spirit – the Spirit of glory – ever keep before me my great privilege of being an heir of Your glory and a citizen of heaven. May my life in its praise and worship of You now be the closest possible approximation to the praise and worship of heaven.

Father, I worship and adore You, through Jesus Christ Your Son. Amen.

Christian Focus Publications

Our mission statement –

STAYING FAITHFUL

In dependence upon God we seek to impact the world through literature faithful to His infallible Word, the Bible. Our aim is to ensure that the Lord Jesus Christ is presented as the only hope to obtain forgiveness of sin, live a useful life and look forward to heaven with Him.

Our books are published in four imprints:

CHRISTIAN
FOCUS

popular works including biographies, commentaries, basic doctrine and Christian living.

CHRISTIAN
HERITAGE

books representing some of the best material from the rich heritage of the church.

MENTOR

books written at a level suitable for Bible College and seminary students, pastors, and other serious readers. The imprint includes commentaries, doctrinal studies, examination of current issues and church history.

CF4•K

children's books for quality Bible teaching and for all age groups: Sunday school curriculum, puzzle and activity books; personal and family devotional titles, biographies and inspirational stories – because you are never too young to know Jesus!

Christian Focus Publications Ltd,
Geanies House, Fearn, Ross-shire,
IV20 1TW, Scotland, United Kingdom.
www.christianfocus.com